THE COMPLETE GUIDE TO POODLES

Tarah Schwartz

Publication Data

Tarah Schwartz

The Complete Guide to Poodles ---- First edition.

Summary: "Successfully raising a Poodles dog from puppy to old age" --- Provided by publisher.

ISBN: 978-1-07311-8-298

[1. Poodles--- Non-Fiction] I. Title.

This book has been written with the published intent to provide accurate and authoritative information in regard to the subject matter included. While every reasonable precaution has been taken in preparation of this book the author and publisher expressly disclaim responsibility for any errors, omissions, or adverse effects arising from the use or application of the information contained inside. The techniques and suggestions are to be used at the reader's discretion and are not to be considered a substitute for professional veterinary care. If you suspect a medical problem with your dog, consult your veterinarian.

Design by Sorin Rădulescu

First paperback edition, 2019

TABLE OF CONTENTS

CHAPTER 17

Advanced Poodle Health and Aging Dog Care

CHAPTER 1
The Poodle

What is a Poodle?

Although Poodles have a reputation as being prissy, high-maintenance dogs, in reality they are athletic, intelligent, eager dogs capable of competing in a variety of sports. Sherri Regalbuto of Just Dogs with Sherri says, "The poodle is an extreme utility breed. Most of the general public sees them in a powder- puff-like image but they are far from what their exterior portrays." They are easy to train and make wonderful companions for active families. Their trainability and high intelligence help them to compete successfully in a variety of sports including agility, obedience, dock diving, and field trials. Their friendly and sensitive nature also allows them to work as service and therapy dogs, as well as in search and rescue.

With three size varieties to choose from, there is a Poodle for everyone, whether you're looking for an active companion or a highly competitive working dog. Their cheerful and regal temperament makes them ideal companions for children and adults alike. Considered the second-smartest dog breed, they learn quickly and can be taught any number of commands or tricks. However, their extreme intelligence must be managed properly to prevent them from finding ways of entertaining themselves. This delightful breed requires plenty of physical and mental exercise, but they make wonderful family members as long as their needs are met.

Poodles are well-known for their fluffy, curly coats, which are usually styled in extravagant, outrageous haircuts. Although the breed has significant grooming requirements, most pet owners find that shorter clips are easier to maintain. The breed does have a reputation as being hypoallergenic, but it should be noted that this is not entirely true. The curly coat of the Poodle sheds less than other coats, so it tends to produce less dander and dead hair than other coat types, but allergens can still be found in the saliva and can stick to clothing, furniture, and other surfaces in the home.

Photo Courtesy of
Rachael Mavroudis

History of the Poodle

The origin of the Poodle is under debate among breed historians. Some say the Poodle descended from the French Barbet breed, while others claim the breed is a descendant of German water dogs. The Fédération Cynologique Internationale, or FCI, is the international organization to which most of France and Germany's kennel clubs belong. The FCI claims that the Poodle hails from France and is a descendant of the Barbet breed. In French, the dogs are referred to as Caniche, which comes from the word cane, or duck. This is a reference to the dogs' history as duck hunters. The American Kennel Club (AKC), Canadian Kennel Club, and British Kennel Club all claim the Poodle originated in Germany and the name comes from the German word pudel, meaning puddle.

Regardless of its place of origin, the Poodle was originally created as a hunting dog. The dogs' intelligence, water-resistant coat, and athletic ability made them excellent hunting companions for both waterfowl and upland bird hunters. The three size varieties were developed after the breed gained popularity in England in the 18th century. The smaller varieties were bred as truffle-hunting dogs and companions. Members of the Victorian middle and upper class soon adopted them as a status symbol.

The haircut the Poodle is most renowned for, the continental clip, began as a way to keep the dog warm during cold-weather hunting trips. The dogs' heavy coat would weigh them down once wet, limiting their agility and speed to retrieve birds. However, shaving the dogs completely allowed the cold water to come into better contact with the dogs' bodies and the dogs would soon become too cold to perform well. Thus, a compromise was made, and Poodle handlers began leaving tufts of hair over the dogs' joints and torsos to insulate them in the cold water. As the breed's popularity grew among the Victorian elite, their once-functional haircuts became exaggerated and were used as a fashion statement.

Although the Poodle's use as a sporting dog has faded, there is a resurgence of breeders and competitors who focus solely on the dogs' working ability. The breed has maintained their trainability and fondness for water sports, so they are rising in popularity in the field once again. As one of the founding breeds in most kennel clubs, they have found success in the show ring since the beginning. Poodles have been frequently awarded Best in Show at the most prestigious dog shows around the world, including Cruft's, the Westminster Kennel Club Dog Show, and the World Dog Show.

*Photo Courtesy of
Kirsten Gendreau*

The Three Varieties

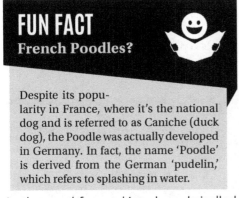

FUN FACT
French Poodles?

Despite its popularity in France, where it's the national dog and is referred to as Caniche (duck dog), the Poodle was actually developed in Germany. In fact, the name 'Poodle' is derived from the German 'pudelin,' which refers to splashing in water.

Although the Poodle is considered to be one breed, they do come in three different size varieties. The breed standard, coat and haircuts, and behavior are similar between all varieties. The three sizes arose from breeders who had a passion for the breed, but not the size of the Standard Poodle. They wanted all of the qualities of the Poodle, but in a more compact package.

As the need for working dogs dwindled and the popularity of companion dogs rose, the Toy Poodle was eventually bred to fill the need for an intelligent, trainable dog that can be carried in one's arms. Technically, the breed standard does allow for the different size varieties to be interbred, but most breeders choose to breed dogs of the same size to maintain consistency in their bloodlines.

The Standard Poodle is the largest of the three varieties. The breed standard states that Standard Poodles must be over 15 inches at the shoulder, but most stand about 22 to 27 inches tall. They usually weigh between 45 and 70 pounds. As larger dogs, Standard Poodles have a slightly shorter life span than the smaller varieties, living an average of about 12 years.

Miniature Poodles are the middle variety, smaller than a Standard Poodle but larger than a Toy. They must be over 10 inches tall at the shoulder, but less than 15. Most Miniatures are between 13 and 15 inches tall at the shoulder. On average, they weigh between 12 and 20 pounds. The average life span of a Miniature Poodle is about 15 years.

Toy Poodles are the smallest variety of Poodle. The breed standard states that they must be less than 10 inches tall at the shoulder. They usually weigh about four to 10 pounds. Their life span is similar to that of the Miniature Poodle.

Physical Characteristics

All three size variations are held to the same standard. There is no difference in body shape or coat, only in size. The breed standard describes the Poodle as having a square appearance. The dog is expected to be roughly as long as it is tall. The ideal Poodle has a moderately rounded skull with a slight but defined stop. The eyes are dark, oval in shape, and give the impression of an intelligent and alert dog. The ears are set at or just below eye level and hang close to the head. The dog's muzzle should long, fine, and straight. The neck should be well-proportioned and long enough to carry the head in a regal fashion. The shape and size of the legs should be in proportion to the dog's overall size. The dog's topline should be level from the top of the shoulder blade to the base of the tail. Poodles have deep chests and moderately wide bodies. The tail is set high on the rear and is carried in an upright position. Poodle tails are typically docked to a length that ensures a balanced appearance. The front legs are strong, straight, and parallel. When viewed from behind, the hind legs should also be straight and parallel, but from the side they should be angled in a way that balances the front end and gives the appearance of a strong, athletic dog.

The Poodle's most renowned physical characteristic is its coat. The coat should be curly and dense with a naturally harsh texture. There are many different styles of clipping that are acceptable in the show ring, depending on a dog's age, and there are even more styles appropriate for pet and sporting dogs. Regardless of the cut, the breed standard states that the coat should be an even and solid color at the skin. Poodles come in a wide variety of colors including blue, gray, silver, brown, café-au-lait, apricot, black, white, and cream. Café-au-lait and liver Poodles should have a brown nose, eye rims, and lips with amber eyes and dark toenails. This is also acceptable in apricots, but it is not desirable. All other colors should have black noses, lips, and eye rims, with dark or self-colored toenails. Parti-colored dogs will be disqualified in the conformation ring, but they are becoming popular as sporting dogs and pets.

Breed Behavioral Characteristics

"The Poodle has a degree of intelligence unlike any other breed. Having been handling and training dogs for over 40 years; I believe that Poodles are hands down the most intelligent."

Sherri Regalbuto
Just dogs with Sherri

One of the most well-known characteristics of the Poodle is the breed's incredible intelligence. Stanley Coren, a professor of canine psychology at the University of British Columbia in Vancouver, Canada, has dedicated his career to studying the intelligence of dogs. Through extensive research and a number of studies, he has determined which breeds are the most intelligent and has ranked them from most intelligent to least according to their trainability and willingness to perform tasks. The Poodle ranks number two on his list and is said to learn new commands after less than five repetitions. Coren considers the Poodle among the brightest breeds of dogs who obey the first command 95 percent of the time or better.

Photo Courtesy of
Jessica Yost

Photo Courtesy of
Jasper Roam

In addition to their intelligence, the sweet and cheerful personality of Poodles makes them excellent companions. Their dedication to their owners and willingness to please make them incredibly easy to train. Their trainability allows them to excel in any dog sport. Poodles of all sizes can be seen competing in obedience, agility, tracking, and even protection. Their history as hunting dogs means they also excel in water sports such as dock diving. Hunters still use them in the field, as well.

There are few differences in behavior between the size varieties, and most differences arise in how they are raised. Standard Poodles tend to be a bit calmer and lower energy than the smaller varieties, but they still need adequate physical and mental exercise to prevent behavioral problems. Miniature and Toy Poodles must be held accountable for their behavior, despite their small size. Without proper training and discipline, they can develop "small dog syndrome," which means they believe they are the leaders of the pack rather than the humans. This can lead to barking, resource guarding, aggression, and nervousness. Since small dogs are often allowed to get away with more bad behavior than larger dogs, they can develop bad behavior quickly. However, with firm, consistent leadership, even smaller Poodles can become well-adjusted, friendly members of the family.

Is a Poodle the Right Fit for You?

"Make sure all family members are on board with getting a new puppy. Have a family discussion and set the ground rules such as: Are they allowed on the couch? Can they eat people food? Where will they sleep?"

Terri L Creech
Bear Cove Standard Poodles

It's easy to fall in love with the regal appearance and outgoing personality of the Poodle, but is it the right breed for your lifestyle? Take time to consider whether or not you're ready and willing to keep up with such an energetic and intelligent dog. In terms of grooming, Poodles are incredibly high-maintenance dogs, so you must be willing to spend the money on regular grooming appointments or learn how to groom your dog properly yourself.

Poodles are incredibly intelligent dogs and require a significant amount of mental and physical stimulation. Without proper exercise for both mind and body, Poodles can develop unwanted and destructive behaviors. Regular training sessions, long walks, and engaging toys and games are excellent ways to keep your Poodle busy. If you are considering adopting a Toy or Miniature Poodle, don't think you are exempt from exercising your dog just because it's small. Even the smallest Poodles will need daily mental and physical exercise. If you aren't willing to dedicate your spare time to training and exercising your Poodle, you may want to consider another breed.

Photo Courtesy of Jessica Minnen

The coats of all three varieties of Poodle require frequent brushing and regular clipping, so they can be quite time consuming to care for. Many Poodle owners opt to have professional groomers take care of their dogs' coats, but this can become costly. Owners who opt to groom their own dogs must learn how to properly and safely use the correct tools to maintain their dogs' coats. Without proper care, coats can become tangled and matted. Mats cannot be brushed out and the dog will need to be shaved to remove them. Severe matting can cause or hide skin conditions. The hair can be pulled, causing discomfort to the dog. In extreme cases, mats can even become so tight that they limit circulation in a dog's limbs, which can lead to permanent injury or even amputation.

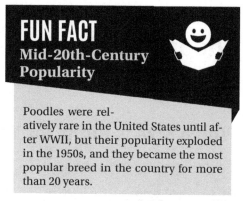

FUN FACT
Mid-20th-Century Popularity

Poodles were relatively rare in the United States until after WWII, but their popularity exploded in the 1950s, and they became the most popular breed in the country for more than 20 years.

Taking care of a Poodle's coat is a commitment that must be taken seriously, so carefully consider this when deciding if the Poodle is the right breed for you.

CHAPTER 2
Choosing a Poodle

Which Size is Right for You?

Photo Courtesy of
Joanna and Rob Sgro

Before deciding whether to buy or adopt your new Poodle, you need to decide which size is right for you and your lifestyle. Each size requires a different type of care, so you need to consider all aspects of your life and your expectations for your new Poodle. With enough physical and mental stimulation, any dog can live in an apartment, but typically smaller dogs do better in small homes while larger dogs thrive with more space. Bigger dogs will also require more food and may cost more to have professionally groomed. You'll also need to consider your intentions for your new puppy. Are you simply looking for a companion or are you looking for a dog to accompany you on long-distance hikes or runs? If you intend to compete in any dog sports, you'll also need to examine the different traits of each size variety and decide which one is best suited for your particular needs.

Consider how much space you have in your home for your new dog. Do you live in a studio apartment in a high-rise building or do you live on a farm in the country? All three sizes can live comfortably in either of these environments, but it may be more difficult to have a large dog in a tiny apartment. Standard Poodles can be excellent apartment dogs, but you may find it difficult to find space for a large crate or space dedicated to your new dog. Some apartment buildings also have weight limits on the dogs they allow to live in the complex. If you live in the country, the wide-open spaces and the predators that live there can be a danger to a Toy Poodle if he is allowed to run loose or escapes. With proper management, a Poodle of any size can thrive in any environment, but it's important to consider the extra work involved.

One of the biggest differences in the three varieties is the cost of raising them. Toy and Miniature Poodles are smaller dogs and will cost less to feed, simply because they eat less than a Standard Poodle. Groomers also typically charge higher prices for larger dogs because they require more time and more work than smaller dogs. Before deciding which type of Poodle you'd like to bring into your home, make sure you can fit the additional costs into your monthly budget.

All dogs require adequate exercise to stay healthy in both mind and body, but it's important to consider how much exercise you're willing to do with your new Poodle. No Poodle will enjoy being a complete couch potato, but a Toy Poodle will likely be more content with less physical exercise than a Miniature or Standard Poodle. On the other hand, if you're a long-distance runner looking for a running buddy, you may want to consider a Standard Poodle, which will be able to keep up with you more easily than a smaller dog. However, if you're more interested in long walks around the neighborhood or hikes around your local trails, any type of Poodle will be happy to be by your side.

The type of lifestyle you lead is an important factor to consider when thinking of adopting a dog. If you travel a lot by plane, you may find it difficult and expensive to travel with a Standard Poodle. If you travel by car, bringing a Poodle of any size will not be too difficult and it may be nice to have company on long drives. Many hotels that are dog-friendly have limits in place that restrict the size of dogs that allowed to stay there. Traveling with dogs always requires more money and attention to detail, but large dogs often require a bit more, so keep this in mind if you're considering adopting a Standard Poodle.

If you intend to compete with your dog, this may also have an impact on what size variety of Poodle you choose to bring into your home. Depending on the sport, large dogs typically compete in a different class than small dogs, so you won't need to worry about competing against larger or smaller dogs. However, some handlers find it easier to train and work with larger dogs since they don't need to bend over as much to maneuver and reward their dogs. Others may find that traveling to competitions is easier with a small dog, so it's worth the extra physical challenge of training a petite dog. If you've competed with dogs in the past, you may already have some idea on what size dog you're looking for, but if you're new to dog sports, you may want to visit a few competitions and speak with the trainers and competitors to get a better idea of what size Poodle is best suited for your sport and your own training style.

Buying vs. Adopting

When deciding whether you should buy your new Poodle from a breeder or adopt one from the shelter, you need to consider what your plans and goals are for the future. If you're looking for a future champion in the show ring, a shelter or breed rescue is probably not where you should be looking. However, if you have fallen in love with the personality and appearance of the breed and simply want a companion, a shelter is a great place to find your new dog.

One of the benefits of adopting from a rescue is the work that has already been put into the dog before you bring it home. Shelters or breed rescues generally put their dogs through rigorous testing to determine their suitability for potential adopters. They are usually tested for friendliness towards people and other animals, food aggression, and trainability. While it's possible that a dog was given up by its previous owner due to behavioral problems, most of the time a dog ends up in a shelter because of the owner's inability to properly care for it. Shelters also usually have dogs of all ages, so if you would prefer to skip the puppy stage, you may be able to find a house-trained adult. If you're interested in competing in dog sports other than conformation, many organizations allow mixed breeds and rescues to compete alongside purebreds. Adopting a dog from a shelter means saving a dog from potential euthanasia, so if you don't need perfect conformation, contact your local shelter or Poodle rescue to see what they have available. Adoption fees typically range up to a few hundred dollars, but the dogs have usually already been spayed or neutered and given the necessary vaccines. If you're on a tight budget, a rescued Poodle may be your best option.

Buying a Poodle from a breeder is probably the best choice if you're looking for a partner in show or sport. Dogs that come from reputable breeders have been health tested, and you can be reasonably confident that outside of any accidents or injuries, you will be bringing home a healthy animal. Breeders will also typically offer much more support throughout your dog's life than you will receive from a shelter or rescue. Breeders know their breed and their dogs better than most, so they are an excellent source of information and advice. You'll also be able to be matched to your ideal dog, which will hopefully lead to a lifetime of happiness for you and your new Poodle. Although most breeders will have only puppies available, some may also have adults that have retired from the show ring or breeding that need new homes. The downside to buying a dog from a reputable breeder is the cost. Although you have the support of the breeder and their contract, you may be spending up to several thousand dollars on your new puppy. Most puppies that come from breeders will only have one or two rounds of vaccines, so you'll also need to plan for the additional cost of vaccines and spaying or neutering.

Photo Courtesy of Juan Barrionuevo

How to Find a Reputable Breeder

The best place to find a reputable breeder is to attend local dog shows and sport competitions, especially if you intend to compete with your new Poodle. By going to the show and seeing the dogs in person, you'll be able to see the dogs in action and speak with their handlers. Most competitors will be happy to discuss their dogs with you. You may find that some Poodles appeal to you more than others, so talk to their handlers and find out where their dogs came from. The individuals handling these dogs may also be breeders, but if they aren't, they will likely be able to recommend the breeder from whom they adopted their dogs.

If your area has a local Poodle breed club, it may also be able to recommend breeders. Many clubs have a list available of the breeders that actively participate in club activities. If your area does not have a local breed club or you do not know how to find one, get in touch with the Poodle Club of America (PCA). Their website has a list of local Poodle clubs, as well as a list of reputable breeders. The PCA website contains contact information for breeders and club officers, as well as information about the individual breed clubs.

Be aware that many reputable breeders may have a waiting list for their puppies. Breeders who consistently produce high-quality dogs and have the appropriate health testing done on their dogs are in high demand and typically only produce one or two litters a year, so you may need to wait

some time before bringing your new puppy home. However, the wait will be worth it. Reputable breeders will not only make sure that you're bringing home a healthy puppy, but they'll make sure you're bringing home the right puppy for you and your family. Quality breeders care about their dogs and want to make sure they are placed in the right homes, so be prepared to be questioned or even interviewed before being approved for adoption.

Whatever you do, do not buy your dog from an advertisement in the local newspaper or an online classifieds website. You should also avoid puppies from pet stores. These breeders do not have the breed's best interest in mind and are typically only in it for the money. Their breeding stock will not have had any health testing done and the health of the puppy you'll be buying may be at risk. In addition to the possibility of bringing home an unwell puppy, these breeders will not offer any guarantees, or have you sign any contracts. This can put you at risk financially, should anything happen to your new puppy.

Photo Courtesy of Tammy Farrington

Health Tests and Certifications

The Orthopedic Foundation for Animals (OFA) is the leading organization in genetic health testing for dogs. For each breed, they recommend a certain series of tests, usually to be performed after the dog has reached maturity at around two years of age. Test results can then be submitted to the OFA to be evaluated by their team of expert veterinarians. Once a dog has been evaluated for all the conditions recommended for its breed, the dog is given a number by the OFA's Canine Health Information Center, or CHIC, and results are entered into their online database. These results are publicly available on the OFA's website and can be found by searching the dog's registered name or individual CHIC number.

For Miniature Poodles, the OFA recommends that dogs undergo a DNA test for Progressive Retinal Atrophy, or PRA. PRA is a degenerative disorder of the retina which eventually leads to blindness. There is no cure, but treatment can slow the degeneration of the retina. Miniature Poodles must also receive an eye test, performed by a veterinarian certified by the American College of Veterinary Ophthalmologists (ACVO). They must also be tested for patellar luxation, which is a condition where the knee cap, or patella, does not stay in its normal place within the groove of the femur. The condition can be quite painful and will worsen as the dog ages. The OFA also requires Miniature Poodles to be tested for hip dysplasia, which is a degenerative disorder of the hip socket that can lead to painful arthritis and joint deterioration.

The OFA recommends that Toy Poodles also undergo DNA testing for Progressive Retinal Atrophy. Like Miniature Poodles, they must also be tested by an ACVO-certified veterinary ophthalmologist. Patellar luxation is also a common condition, so Toy Poodles must also be tested for that disorder after one year of age, but unlike Miniature Poodles, they do not need to be tested for hip dysplasia. Once owners submit results from all three tests, Toy Poodles can then receive their CHIC number.

Standard Poodles must also undergo testing by an ACVO-certified veterinary ophthalmologist but do not need to be tested for PRA. As hip dysplasia is common in this variety, owners must submit x-rays to be evaluated by the OFA. The third test can be one of three, chosen by the owner or breeder. One of the options is a thyroid evaluation, performed by an OFA-approved laboratory. Dogs may also be tested for Sebaceous Adenitis, which is a disease in which the sebaceous glands of the skin become inflamed, leading to severe hair loss. This test must be performed by an OFA-approved dermatopathologist. The third option is a congenital or advanced cardiac exam. Results of this exam must then be sent to the OFA for approval.

Breeder Contracts and Guarantees

Contracts and guarantees are an important part of the purchase of a purebred dog. This legally binding contract ensures that both you and the breeder are protected financially if things don't go as planned. Typically, the contract guarantees that the dog you're buying is healthy and has received proper veterinary care up until the moment it leaves the breeder's possession. If you're buying a pet, rather than a show dog, there may also be a clause which requires you to spay or neuter the dog at the appropriate age. If you're buying a show or performance dog, there may be a clause preventing you from spaying or neutering the dog unless approved by the breeder. The contract may also include a "happiness clause," which simply means that if the puppy does not meet your expectations or if things do not work out, the puppy may be returned to the breeder. In this case, you may or may not receive a refund. Be sure to read your contract carefully and thoroughly and ask questions if there is anything you don't understand. Reputable breeders are only interested in the well-being of their dogs, so be sure that you understand what the breeder expects from you and vice versa.

Choosing the Perfect Puppy

"The first thing a person needs to do is sit with their family and discuss where their new Poodle family member will fit in. Do they need a jogging partner, camping and hiking buddy, Service Dog or other working job? Or will this new member be a pet and couch potato? This is VERY important to know before meeting with your Breeder/Rescue so that you are able to communicate your family's needs for energy and temperament."

LeeAnna Springer
Springer Clan Standard Poodles

When faced with a litter of adorable Poodle puppies, making a choice can be a difficult task. Before you make a final decision, there is a lot to consider. A puppy's appearance will be the first thing you notice about it, but it should receive the least amount of consideration. A dog's color or coat pattern will not have any effect on the dog as a companion and will only need to be considered if you are showing the dog in conformation, where certain colors and patterns will be faulted.

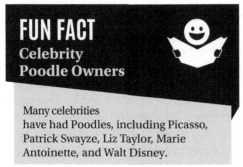

FUN FACT

Celebrity Poodle Owners

Many celebrities have had Poodles, including Picasso, Patrick Swayze, Liz Taylor, Marie Antoinette, and Walt Disney.

You'll first need to decide whether you would prefer a male or female puppy. If you have other dogs, you may need to consider what gender your current pets get along with best. Some female dogs may prefer the company of males, while others display aggressive behavior toward male dogs. Male dogs may or may not get along with other males, especially if they are unneutered, so it's important to know your current dogs' preferences before choosing a puppy. If you have no other pets and no preference, you can let your breeder help you choose your new Poodle based on other traits, rather than just gender.

The most important aspect in choosing a puppy is determining what your long-term goals are for your new dog. If you plan on showing the dog or competing in sports, you'll need a dog that is suited for competition, rather than one who lacks drive or perfect conformation. If you aren't sure what sport you'd like to compete in, but you know you'd like to show the dog, discuss this with the breeder and they may be able to find a dog that you can explore your options with. If you simply want a companion, let your breeder know. Puppies intended to be just pets often cost less than show dogs, and breeders generally have a clause in their contracts requiring pets to be spayed or neutered, whereas show dogs are usually kept intact.

Breeders spend more time with their dogs than anyone, so they are the best resource to consult when deciding on a puppy. They'll have the best idea of each puppy's personality and how its conformation and physical ability are developing. Many breeders may be unwilling to let future show-ring stars go to pet homes, so be honest and thorough in discussing your needs with your breeder. If you have certain goals in mind for your new dog, tell your breeder so they can help you choose the ideal puppy. As the puppies age, the breeder will be able to determine which puppies are best suited for show homes and which will end up in pet homes, so it may be several weeks after the puppies are born before any future adopters are allowed to choose.

Tips for Adopting a Poodle

All-breed rescue organizations are a great place to find a Poodle, but you may also be able to find a breed-specific rescue in your area. A breed rescue, such as a Poodle rescue, will focus on one breed, so they will only work with Poodles or Poodle mixes. The volunteers involved in breed rescues are passionate about their breed and they will be a great resource in finding the perfect Poodle for you and your family.

Photo Courtesy of Whitney Charisma

When applying for adoption, you'll likely have to fill out a questionnaire and undergo a brief interview. Some rescues also have a volunteer come to your home to make sure it's a safe environment for a dog. Don't worry, if they find any problems, they'll likely give you a chance to fix the issue rather than deny your adoption application. The intention is not to invade your privacy, but to make sure they're placing the dog in the appropriate home. Rescue staff and volunteers want to see their dogs find their forever homes and they can only do that when they know enough about potential adopters to match them to their ideal dog. These interviews are also a great opportunity for you to ask any questions you may have about the breed or the specific dog you're interested in. If you don't have a specific dog in mind, you can discuss what you're looking for in a dog to see if they have a Poodle that might suit your needs.

If you have any hesitations about adopting a Poodle, consider fostering a rescue Poodle before committing to adoption. Many rescues would rather have their dogs experience life in a home rather than in a kennel, so they often have fostering opportunities available. You'll have to undergo the same questioning and perhaps a home check before being approved to foster, but it will give you a chance to get to know the breed before making the decision to adopt. It's not unusual for foster dogs to become "foster fails" when their foster family falls in love with them, so if you meet your perfect match, don't be afraid to sign the adoption papers.

CHAPTER 3
Preparing Your Home for Your New Poodle

"Poodles can pretty much fit into any family environment, any level of exercise, calm families, or high-energy families. They are pretty much a dog that can adjust to any situation."

Mary Ann Riess
Vision Red Standard Poodles

Adjusting Your Current Pets and Children

Bringing a new family member home can be a stressful experience, especially if you have other pets or children. Properly introducing your new Poodle to your family is essential to the beginning of their life-long relationships. Occasionally, not everyone gets along right away, and it may take time to develop a good relationship, so don't give up if the first day doesn't go as planned. No matter what, for the first several weeks after bringing your puppy home, do not leave him with other pets or children unattended. Poodle puppies, especially Toy and Miniature Poodles, are small and can easily be injured. Your other pets or kids may not mean to hurt the puppy, but accidents can and do happen.

When introducing your new Poodle puppy to current pets, it may be advisable to introduce them on neutral ground. Some pets can become territorial with new animals, so to prevent any issues you should try to introduce them away from your current pets' territory. Outside spaces such as a front yard or garage work well. If weather doesn't permit outdoor introductions, try using a room that your pet doesn't spend much time in, such as a dining room or laundry room.

Before you bring the puppy home, spend some time explaining to your children the proper way to interact with a dog. Once they see the puppy, they can easily become excited and it will be impossible to try to explain the rules at that point. This discussion is for their safety as well as the puppy's. An excited child can easily play too roughly with a delicate puppy and injure it, but it's possible the child may also scare the puppy. A scared puppy may feel the need to protect himself and may bite the child. Puppies also bite during play, especially when they are playing with a rambunctious child. Explain to the children that slow, gentle touches are best and discourage smaller children from attempting to pick the puppy up.

Supervision is key to preventing accidents. It can be a hassle to monitor every interaction between your new puppy and your current pets and children, but it's better than the alternative. Most fights between animals and accidents between animals and children can be prevented if you keep an eye out for the warning signs. If at any time the dog, child, or other animal seem uncomfortable, it's time to separate them. Short introductory sessions a few times a day will help everyone adjust to each other, while allowing everyone their own safe space as well.

Photo Courtesy of
Emil Friberg

Dangerous Things that Dogs Might Eat

Photo Courtesy of Joanna and Rob Sgro

Puppies explore their world with their mouths and the average household is full of potential dangers. Before bringing your Poodle puppy home, you need to go through your house to make sure that any potential dangers are either removed or placed out of the puppy's reach.

If you have houseplants, you need to make sure that they are nontoxic to dogs. Some plants can cause serious digestive or neurological problems, or even death, so it's important to do your research. If you can't bear to part with your favorite toxic plants, just make sure they are placed somewhere that your puppy will not be able to reach them. If you have an outdoor garden, the same rule applies there as well. Any toxic plants need to be removed from your yard or fenced off.

Trash cans can be incredibly tempting to a curious puppy. They're full of interesting smells and delicious treats, but they can be full of danger as well. Cooked bones, plastic wrappers, and used household supplies can all be dangerous or even deadly if ingested. If your trash can can't be hidden inside of a cabinet, try shopping for a can that is large enough and heavy enough that it can't be tipped over. Some trash cans can even be locked when you're not using them, so use your best judgment to decide what will work best for your situation.

If you have children, have a discussion with them about keeping their toys out of the puppy's reach. Puppies can easily confuse children's toys for their own, and small toys, such as cars or figurines, can be gulped down in the blink of an eye. Making sure your puppy doesn't get into your kids' toys will prevent a potential intestinal blockage, and it will also prevent disappointment and resentment when your kids discover the puppy has eaten their favorite toy.

Other Household Dangers

Although Poodles were bred to be water dogs, pools can be incredibly dangerous to an unsupervised Poodle puppy. If you have a fenced-in pool, make sure the puppy can't squeeze through the fence into the pool area. You may need to repair holes or line the bottom half of the fence before allowing your puppy into the backyard. If your pool is not fenced in, your Poodle must be supervised at all times. It takes only a second for a dog to slip over the edge and into the water, so keep a close eye on your puppy any time he's in the yard. There are products available that act as a ramp for animals who have fallen into pools, so you may want to consider purchasing one as a backup in case something happens. Some animals panic enough after falling in that they may not be able to find the ramp, but it at least gives them a way out if they can find it.

Care must be taken to ensure that all doors and gates in the house and yard are secured. It takes only a second for a puppy to slip out an open door. The world can be a dangerous place for an unaccompanied Poodle puppy, especially the smaller varieties. If your Poodle escapes the house without identification, he can become lost or taken in as a stray. If he wanders into the street, passing cars may have difficulty spotting such a small animal and he may be hit. Predators, such as coyotes, bobcats, or even other dogs also present a danger to Poodle puppies. To prevent tragedy, it's best to make sure that all doors and gates have been closed tightly before allowing your poodle into the room or yard. When you leave your puppy in his designated area, it's a good idea to double-check all crate doors and gate latches before leaving, just to make sure that the puppy is safe and secure in his own space.

Long flights of stairs can also be a hazard to a clumsy puppy. While it's unlikely that your puppy will be severely injured if he tumbles down a few steps off the porch, if you have long flights of stairs in your home or live in an apartment building with long flights of stairs, take care to keep your puppy away from them. Never allow your puppy to wander freely in the area without supervision. It's best if you can place a barrier, such as a pressure-mounted baby gate, at the top of the stairs to prevent your puppy from accidentally falling down the stairs.

Preparing a Space for Your Poodle Inside

Before you bring your Poodle home, you'll need to prepare a safe and secure area for him to stay. Allowing your puppy access to the entire house right away will only lead to house-training difficulties and chewed-up furniture and personal items. Your puppy's area should be separated from the rest of the home with a baby gate, or you can use a wire or plastic playpen. Try to choose an area with easy-to-clean floors such as tile or laminate flooring, such as a spare bathroom, laundry room, or section of the kitchen. A room that is near most of the action in the home, but still allows the puppy some quiet time, is ideal. Your puppy's area should not be too large. During house-training, you don't want the puppy to have too much space without supervision. The more frequently the puppy is allowed to eliminate inside the house without correction, the more difficult house-training will be.

As you set up the room, get down on the puppy's level to spot any potential dangers. The area must be thoroughly puppy proofed before you bring your Poodle home. If there are any electrical cords, houseplants, or furniture that can be easily knocked over, remove them or place them out of the puppy's reach. You'll also need to make sure that any cabinets cannot be opened by a curious puppy. Child-proof cabinet locks work well with even the nosiest puppies. Make sure all doors and gates are secure. Poodle puppies, especially Toy Poodles, can squeeze through small gaps, so make sure the area is secure before bringing your puppy home.

As you set up the area, consider lining the floor with absorbent puppy pads. Accidents are bound to happen, and puppy pads can make cleanup a bit easier. Be sure to keep an eye on your puppy if you plan on using puppy pads. If you notice him chewing on them or tearing them up, you need to remove them immediately. You'll also want to think about where you place your puppy's bed and dishes. Placing the bed in the quietest corner of the space will allow the puppy to have a safe space to retreat to if he gets overwhelmed during the first few days in his new home. If you plan on crate training your puppy, you can place his bed inside of his crate. Some owners choose to cover the crate with a blanket or crate cover to give their dogs a bit more privacy. Your puppy's food and water dishes need to be placed some distance away from his bedding to prevent him from soiling his bed if he knocks over any dishes. It's a good idea to keep dishes away from the entrance of the area. The puppy may become excited when you come home or let him out and he may knock over his dishes accidentally.

Preparing Outside Spaces

As with your Poodle's space indoors, you need to get on his level outdoors and check for any potential dangers. Walk the fence line to be sure there aren't any holes or loose boards that could allow a puppy to squeeze through. The smaller varieties of Poodle are especially good at squeezing through tight spaces to escape. Keeping your puppy in is just as important as keeping potential predators out. Wild animals such as coyotes and bobcats can easily snatch up your puppy if given the opportunity. If your fence has wide gaps, as in a wrought iron or metal fence, you may want to consider lining the bottom half of the fence with wire fencing with smaller gaps, such as chicken wire. Just make sure to attach the chicken wire securely to the fence itself, so the puppy can't pull it away.

Photo Courtesy of
Bec Bland

As with your houseplants, you need to go through your yard and make sure your plants are nontoxic to dogs. If you have flower beds or a vegetable garden, you may want to fence them off to prevent your puppy from digging up your plants. A garden can be a dangerous place for a puppy, but a puppy can just as easily destroy a garden full of plants or flowers. A small fence or barrier should be enough to keep a curious puppy away from your precious plants. The products you use to keep your yard and garden looking their best can also be a danger to your puppy. If you usually use chemical weed-killer or fertilizer, you may want to examine the ingredients and look for more dog-friendly options.

Supplies

FUN FACT
Historical Hounds

Dogs resembling Poodles have been found on Roman and Egyptian artifacts and tombs dating back to the first century B.C.

It's important to make sure you have all of the necessary supplies before you bring your new Poodle home. Introducing a new member of the family will be stressful anyway, so you don't want the added stress of forgetting to buy food for your puppy. Make your list of the essentials and check it several times before you bring the puppy home, just to make sure you haven't missed anything. Some items, such as toys, clothing, and grooming supplies, are not necessary right away, and you can consider buying them at a later time.

One of the most important items you need for your puppy is a comfortable, securely fitted collar with identification. You may not know the exact size your puppy will wear, but depending on which variety of Poodle you have adopted, you can make a fairly accurate guess. Most collars are adjustable and can adjust several inches if necessary. For the identification, some owners prefer tags, but others prefer metal collar plates. Name plates do not jingle like tags do, but sometimes it's nice to be able to hear where your puppy is based on the noise from his identification tags. You'll also need a leash, preferably between four and six feet long. Extendable leashes are not recommended while training your dog, but you can consider one later on in your training when you know what to expect from your dog. You'll also need food and water dishes and a comfortable bed. Remember, puppies love to chew, so it may not be a good idea to spend a large amount of money on your Poodle's first bed since he may just chew it up. Try to find one with a removable cover as it will make washing much easier. There will be times where you will need to wash the whole bed, but it will last longer if you can just wash the cover on occasion. Some dogs also enjoy burrowing under blankets when they sleep. You may want to consider buying a small, inexpensive blanket for your puppy to see if he enjoys the security of being covered while he sleeps. Many stores sell relatively inexpensive fleece blankets and if your puppy chews it up, it can be easily replaced.

When you're shopping for supplies, you'll also need to consider how you plan on house-training your puppy. Disposable absorbent puppy pads are a great item to have on hand. They're great for lining crates and play-pens. If you plan on using an indoor potty patch, you may also want to consider buying one at this time. If you would prefer your dog only uses the outdoors, consider buying a bell for the door. There are quite a few companies that make bells designed to hang from a doorknob that can be nudged or pawed at when your dog wants to go outside.

There are items that make living with a puppy easier, but they aren't entirely necessary. If you want to encourage your puppy to play with toys, consider buying a few different kinds to see what he prefers. Plastic or wooden puzzle toys are also a great way to encourage your puppy to use his mind and keep him busy while you do household chores. Grooming supplies, such as shampoo, combs, nail clippers, and toothbrushes can also make puppy care a little easier. Even if you don't plan on grooming your Poodle yourself, it can still be nice to have the supplies on hand should you notice your puppy's coat getting tangled, or if he manages to find a mud puddle on your morning walk.

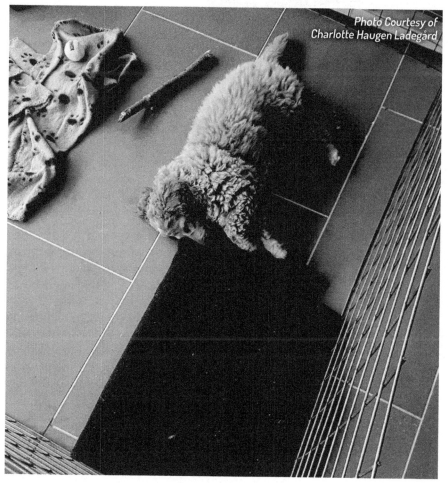

Photo Courtesy of
Charlotte Haugen Ladegård

CHAPTER 4

Bringing Home Your New Poodle

The Importance of Having a Plan

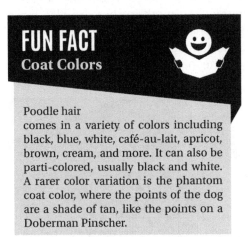

FUN FACT
Coat Colors

Poodle hair comes in a variety of colors including black, blue, white, café-au-lait, apricot, brown, cream, and more. It can also be parti-colored, usually black and white. A rarer color variation is the phantom coat color, where the points of the dog are a shade of tan, like the points on a Doberman Pinscher.

Bringing your new Poodle puppy home will be exciting and stressful for both you and the dog. If you don't have a plan and thoroughly prepare for the arrival of your new family member, the stress may leave a negative impression on you both. Having a plan will not only ease this transition, but it will give you more time to spend bonding with your puppy, rather than rushing around trying to prepare. Forgetting to set up your puppy's designated area, or not having the correct supplies on hand can set your new relationship off on the wrong foot. However, if you take the time to prepare your home and make a plan for the first few days with your new dog, you'll be able to devote more of your time on your new puppy.

It's also important to have realistic expectations about the first few days and weeks with your new Poodle. Remember, whether you're bringing home a puppy or an adult dog, moving into a new home with a new family can be a worrying time for the dog, so things may not go as smoothly as you'd like. Sharon Heath of Kokopelli Standard Poodles says, "Depending on the age of the Poodle you are bringing into your home, it could be missing its siblings and will need to transfer that connection to you. If it's an older pup, it could be scared, as they do go through a fear stage at about 12 to 16 weeks. An older poodle may be confused if they suddenly lost their previous owner, and that takes a while, but they fall in love very easy with kindness." No matter what happens, be patient and consistent in your training and your new Poodle will settle into his new home in no time.

The Ride Home

Before you pick up your new Poodle from the breeder or shelter, you need to consider how you're going to get him home. Safety should be your top priority, so consider your options carefully and prepare accordingly. If you're bringing your Poodle home by car, he should be properly restrained for your safety as well as his. Letting the puppy ride unrestrained in the back seat or in a passenger's lap is not a good idea. An unrestrained puppy can easily jump into the driver's lap or onto the floor, potentially causing an accident. In the case of an accident caused by another driver or outside force, an unrestrained puppy can be seriously injured or even

Photo Courtesy of Asya Semenovich

killed in a wreck. He may also escape the car and flee out of fear, so to prevent any potential tragedies, it's best to use some sort of restraint system.

Many Poodle owners keep crates in the cargo areas or back seats of their cars. This is one of the safest methods of transporting a dog in a car and it also provides a certain level of comfort for insecure or frightened dogs. The crates can be covered if the dog prefers the seclusion, and they can be easily removed and cleaned out if the dog becomes carsick. Choose your crate depending on the size of your Poodle. Hard-sided plastic crates or wire crates are excellent choices. Putting a blanket or towel in the crate will give your dog something comfortable to sit on that is easily washed if he soils it. If your breeder or shelter allows it, you might want to put a small towel, blanket, or toy from the dog's previous home in his crate to comfort him during this stressful time. Crates are also excellent choices for dogs that are fearful about riding in cars. Some dogs may try to bolt once the car door is opened and a crate allows you to open the car door and prepare for your dog's exit without worrying about him running off. A crate is probably the best option for your puppy's first ride home and once he has more training and experience riding in cars, you can decide whether you'd like to continue using the crate or try something different.

Seat belts are also a great option for older, more experienced travelers. Doggy seat belts consist of a short leash which attaches to the seat-belt buckle on one end and the dog's harness at the other. Be sure to always use a harness with a seat-belt attachment, rather than a collar. In the case of an accident, a harness will spread the pressure out over the dog's entire chest, rather than just his neck. A seat-belt leash attached to a collar can seriously injure or kill a dog. The downside to doggy seat belts is that the dog will be able to soil the car's seats and floors if he becomes carsick. He may also bring sticks, dirt, or sand into the car from the outside. Owners who choose to use seat belts with their dogs often invest in seat covers to prevent any permanent damage to their car's seats.

If crates and seat belts aren't your style, you may want to consider metal or fabric barriers for your car. These barriers are usually either pressure mounted or attach to the car's seats. They can be used to keep your dog in the cargo area or back seat and prevent him from jumping into the front seat. Many owners also use seat or cargo area covers in combination with barriers to keep their car clean. These are an excellent choice for well-behaved dogs who can be trusted not to chew up your car's seats or bolt out the door when you arrive at your destination. The only downside to barriers is that if you are in an accident, your dog may still be injured if he is thrown into the barrier or sides of the car. If the windows are damaged, he may also be able to escape and run away. Carefully consider all of your options and decide which works best for you and your car.

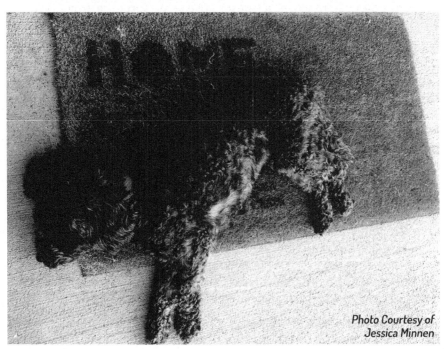

Photo Courtesy of Jessica Minnen

The First Night Home

Your Poodle's first night home will be stressful, and it's unlikely you'll get a restful night's sleep. Your puppy will be nervous and frightened, spending the night in a new home away from his littermates. Keep your expectations low for the first few nights, as it may take some time for your puppy to settle in. Thorough preparation before bringing your puppy

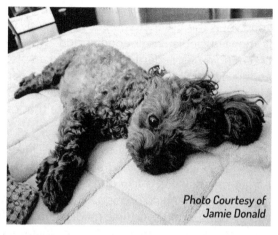

Photo Courtesy of Jamie Donald

home and before putting your puppy to bed will make a significant difference in how well your first night goes.

Decide where your puppy will be sleeping for the first night. In the distant future, you may want your dog to sleep in bed with you, or on a dog bed in your bedroom, but that's not a wise choice for the first night. Until your dog is fully house-trained, you'll need to keep him in a small, secure area during the night to discourage him from eliminating inside the house. Some owners choose to keep a crate in their bedroom for this purpose, while others set the puppy up in a crate or playpen in another part of the house. Some puppies may find comfort in being near you during the night, while others will cry regardless, so it's up to you to decide where your puppy will sleep.

Be sure to take your puppy outside as late as possible before going to bed. You'll probably be waking up a few times during the night to take him out anyway, but the later you take him out, the longer you can sleep between trips outside. Remember, your puppy will be able to go one hour for every month of his age between potty breaks, so if your puppy is three months old, he'll be able to go three hours before needing to go outside. It may be difficult in the beginning to determine whether your puppy is crying because he needs to go outside or if he's just upset, but keeping track of his potty breaks will help. If in doubt, take him out. In the following nights, try to take him out around the same time to establish a routine. Soon, your puppy will understand that it's bedtime after this last trip outside, and he should quiet down sooner as he adjusts to his new schedule.

Choosing a Vet and the First Visit

If you do not already have a regular vet, the best resource for finding a good vet is the breeder you got your puppy from. Their veterinarian is likely knowledgeable about Poodles and aware of common problems with the breed. If your breeder isn't local, you can also ask friends, family, or other Poodle owners in the area for their recommendations. If you prefer a more holistic approach, the American Holistic Veterinary Medical Association has a list of veterinarians on their website that can be searched by location as well as specialty.

Your puppy's first visit to the vet will likely be quite short and simple. Your puppy will be weighed and given a physical examination. The veterinarian may ask you a few questions regarding your Poodle's diet and eating habits. Depending on his age, your puppy may also receive one or more vaccinations as a deworming medication. The first visit is a great opportunity to get to know the team that will be taking care of your dog, so if you have any questions, don't hesitate to ask. The veterinarian or veterinary technician will be happy to discuss any concerns you may have. It's also a great time to discuss future appointments for vaccinations or spaying or neuter-

ing, so if you have any questions about these procedures, this is an ideal time to ask them.

The key to making this first vet visit a success is not to worry about it. Dogs can sense your nervousness, so if you are tense, your puppy will pick up on your anxiety and may become fearful. Remember, the veterinarian and technicians are professionals and handle dogs of all shapes, sizes, and ages every day. Your puppy is in caring hands, so trust your veterinary team and try not to let your nervousness affect your puppy's behavior. Take a few deep breaths, hold the leash loosely, and relax. If your puppy does seem nervous in his new surroundings, try not to coddle him. This will make him believe there is a reason to be nervous and may make his behavior worse. If you act as though there is nothing to worry about, your puppy will follow your lead. The first vet visit should leave a positive impression on your puppy, since he will likely be visiting them regularly for the rest of his life.

Puppy Classes

If you've never trained a dog before, or you would like a little help, puppy classes are a great option. Depending on your area, they may be offered by independent trainers, pet stores, or even a local shelter or rescue. The prices of such classes will depend on where they're held and how long the classes are. Most puppy classes take place once or twice a week for several weeks. Some places will also have different levels, so once your puppy completes his first series of classes, he can move on to the next. Each level will allow you to work on more advanced skills. Puppy classes are also a great way to socialize your Poodle and introduce him to new people and dogs in a controlled environment. If you encounter any problems along the way, your trainer will be right there to help you. Puppy classes are also a great place to meet other dog owners, who may want to set up playdates outside of class.

If your new Poodle has any behavioral problems, or you're not sure if you're ready for a group class, most trainers offer private one-on-one lessons. Lessons can typically be held at your home, the trainer's facility, or at a local park. Private lessons are generally more expensive than group lessons, but you do get the trainer's complete attention during that time. If you're bringing home a rescue dog, or have allowed your puppy to develop bad habits, a private training session may be exactly what you need to get your dog back on the right track. The trainer will be able to guide you through your problems and help you set goals to mark your progress. If you're comfortable, you may be able to transition into group lessons after a few private sessions with the trainer.

Cost Breakdown for The First Year

Although dogs do not care whether they live in a modest environment or a mansion, it's important to carefully consider whether you are able to provide the appropriate level of care for your dog. This breakdown is just an estimate of the yearly cost of raising a Poodle puppy. The specific amounts may vary based on the size variety you choose, as well as the area you live in and how much you're willing to spend on your new dog. Your local pet store or favorite online retailer likely has a variety of supplies in a range of prices, so you'll be able to choose according to your budget. The bigger the Poodle, the more food it will need to consume, so consider how much you can spend on your dog's diet when choosing what to feed him. Routine veterinary care will likely be your highest cost, so be sure to set aside enough money for vaccines and spaying or neutering.

Mandatory Expenses	Cost Estimate
Food	$150 - $900
Food and Water Dishes	$10 - $50
Treats	$50 - $150
Toys	$20 - $200
Collars and Leashes	$10 - $100
Crate	$25 - $100
Dog Beds	$25 - $100
Vaccines and Routine Veterinary Care	$100 - $350
Heartworm Testing	$10 - $35
Heartworm Prevention	$25 - $125
Flea and Tick Prevention	$40 - $200
Spaying or Neutering	$150 - $600
Puppy Classes	$200 - $500
Totalvvv	$815 - $2730

In addition to routine veterinary care, supplies, and food, you need to set aside a certain amount of money in case of emergencies. Accidents cannot always be prevented, so you must be prepared for the potential costs involved. Emergency veterinary care can reach into the thousands, so you need to know how much you are willing and able to spend should something happen to your dog.

Grooming and boarding can also be expensive, depending on your area and the size variety you have adopted. Larger dogs, such as Standard Poodles, are typically more expensive to groom and board than smaller dogs. This is an area where money can be saved, however, if your budget is tight. Learning to groom your Poodle yourself can save you thousands of dollars over the course of your dog's life. You can also ask friends or family to take care of your dog while you travel, saving you the cost of leaving him at a boarding facility or kennel. If possible, you may also be able to bring your dog with you. No matter what you choose to do, it's important to consider these potential costs before signing the adoption papers.

Possible Expenses	Cost Estimate
Professional Grooming	$300 - $1000
Emergency Veterinary Services	$200 - $1000+
Pet Sitting or Boarding	$15 - $50+ per day

Remember, adopting a dog is a serious responsibility and you need to carefully consider whether this is something you can afford. Dogs don't need fancy collars and beds, but they do need proper veterinary care and a balanced diet, so make sure you can afford the basics before committing to adoption. Some owners choose to keep a separate savings account just for their dogs in case of emergencies, so you may want to consider setting aside a small amount every month so you will have it should tragedy strike.

CHAPTER 5
Being a Puppy Parent

Standing by Your Expectations

Photo Courtesy of
Juan Barrionuevo

When bringing your Poodle puppy home, it's important to consider your expectations for the following weeks and even months. Some puppies adapt quickly and develop a daily routine rather quickly, while others may struggle a bit in the change from living with their littermates to living with a human family. You need to keep your expectations low in order to make the best of a complicated and potentially difficult situation. Do not expect your puppy to sleep through the night during the first several weeks and do not expect house-training to progress quickly. If things go well, you can celebrate your puppy's progress, but if training and socializing take longer than you expected, don't be disappointed.

It can be easy to become frustrated with an energetic, unfocused puppy, but patience and understanding are key during the first few months. Terri Creech of Bear Cove Standard Poodles advises, "This puppy's world has been turned upside down. Find a routine and stick to it." If you find yourself becoming frustrated or upset with your puppy's progress, don't hesitate to contact a professional trainer immediately. A trainer can help you solve your puppy's problem behaviors before they become unmanageable. They may also be able to help you develop a training plan and offer advice to help you reach your goals with your new family member.

How to Crate Train

Even if you don't plan on using a crate when your Poodle reaches adulthood, crate training is an essential part of your dog's education. If you take your dog to the vet, groomer, or boarding kennel, he will need to know how to wait patiently in a crate without excessive barking or destructive behavior. A dog with poor crate manners is a danger to himself and others. He may become fearful and nervous, or even aggressive when placed inside a crate for the first time during a stressful situation. Dogs with no crate experience may destroy bedding or soil the crate. They may also try to escape the crate by chewing or digging, potentially caus-

Photo Courtesy of Joanna and Rob Sgro

ing permanent damage to their teeth and nails. It's unfair to expect your groomer or veterinary team to deal with this behavior when it can be prevented with regular training at home. Additionally, crate training can make house-training progress much quicker, with fewer messes and setbacks.

If your Poodle is not used to spending time in a crate, he may become upset at first. To prevent this, try encouraging him to enter the crate on his own by tossing a few treats inside. Praise him whenever he enters, especially if he stays inside for any amount of time. As he becomes more comfortable, you can begin shutting the door behind him, if only for a few seconds at first. Praise him excessively for remaining calm and quiet. Slowly increase the amount of time you leave him in the crate. As he becomes more comfortable, you can try offering him his favorite chew treats or toys as a reward and to keep him distracted while inside of the crate. Until you know how your Poodle will behave in a crate, it's best not to leave him unsupervised for any significant amount of time until you know he's not a danger to himself. Crating your puppy while you do household chores is a great opportunity for your dog to become more comfortable in the crate since he can still see and hear you.

Once you get to know your new Poodle better, you can use your best judgment as to whether you should leave beds, blankets, or toys in the crate with your dog. Some dogs may become destructive out of frustration or boredom, but it may comfort less destructive dogs. Crating your dog while you work around the house is a great opportunity to test your Poodle to see if he can be trusted with items in his crate. If you see him chewing or attempting to rip his bed or blankets, remove them immediately. If this were to happen without your supervision, he could accidentally swallow a piece, potentially choking or creating an intestinal blockage. If he remains calm and relaxed with items in his crate, you can begin leaving them inside for longer amounts of time. It's not recommended to leave food or water inside your dog's crate, as he can accidentally knock over the bowls and make a mess of himself and the crate. If he is still in the process of house-training, it can throw off his daily routine and may encourage him to soil the crate before his next bathroom break.

Photo Courtesy of
Susan Ruderman

Chewing

One of the most destructive and dangerous bad habits a dog can develop is chewing. Dogs who develop this habit may chew on shoes, children's toys, furniture, and even walls. Their destruction can create tension within the family and possibly even resentment toward the new puppy. Chewing will not only cause problems among family members, but it can also put your Poodle's life at risk. Dogs who chew may purposefully or inadvertently swallow pieces of whatever they are chewing. Splinters of wood, chunks of plastic, or pieces of drywall can all become intestinal blockages. Without surgical intervention, an intestinal blockage can be fatal.

However, puppies do not chew on inappropriate items because they want to be bad. Much like human babies, they explore their world by putting things in their mouth. As they begin teething, chewing can help relieve some of the discomfort, so they may pick up the nearest object to chew on, even if it does not belong to them. Puppies who chew must be supervised at all times when out of their puppy-proofed designated area or crate. Consistency in correction is the only way to solve this habit. If your puppy is allowed to chew on shoes when he's not supervised, but gets scolded when in your presence, he'll only learn not to chew when you're around.

There are many ways to handle a dog who chews. Your local pet store or favorite online retailer likely has a variety of sprays that can be used on inappropriate items such as furniture. Typically, the sprays are either an extremely sour flavor, such as apple, or a spicy flavor, such as pepper. The unpleasant taste will discourage your dog from chewing on the item that has been sprayed. Remember, you will likely need to reapply the spray after a

NOT-SO-FUN FACTS
Health Problems

Sadly, purebred Poodles are prone to a wide variety of health problems. Different sizes of Poodles are prone to different health problems, but conditions that may affect Poodles include:
- Addison's Disease
- Cushing's Disease
- Bloat
- Hip dysplasia
- Epilepsy
- Patellar luxation
- Hypothyroidism
- Legg-Perthes Disease
- Sebaceous Adenitis (SA)
- Progressive Retinal Atrophy (PRA)
- Optic nerve hypoplasia
- Von Willebrand's Disease

certain period of time to make sure your dog understands that he shouldn't chew on those items. Another option is to provide your dog with appropriate objects to chew on such as toys or treats. If you catch your dog in the act, rather than punish him, simply swap out the items and praise him for chewing on the correct object. There is a huge selection of chew toys on the market, from toys that can be filled with food to more natural choices, such as hooves and antlers. There are even toys designed to be put in the freezer when not in use to provide a cooling sensation for teething puppies with sore gums. It may take some trial and error to find what type of toy your Poodle prefers, but once you do, reward him with praise every time he chooses the toy over the shoe. However, it should be noted that even chew toys can be chewed down or have pieces broken off that can become choking hazards or potential intestinal blockages, so always keep a close eye on your puppy's toys.

Growling and Barking

Although it may be cute to see a tiny, fluffy puppy barking and growling aggressively, this type of behavior must be discouraged from the start. As the dog grows, the behavior can escalate if it's not corrected, resulting in a difficult and potentially dangerous dog. Not all dogs who growl or bark at other people or dogs are acting out of aggression though. It's not uncommon for fearful or shy dogs to react aggressively out of fear, and once they see that their behavior keeps others at a distance, they're more likely to repeat it. This is why socialization is so important. The more people and dogs your puppy meets, the more confident he will be in new situations, making him less likely to react out of fear or aggression.

If your puppy growls or barks at a stranger or another dog, you need to correct this behavior immediately. A sharp clap, stomp, or yelp will surprise and distract the dog, hopefully discouraging the unwanted behavior. Never yell or hit your dog as a correction. Not only can you traumatize the dog, but in his escalated state, he may react aggressively toward you out of fear. It's also unhelpful to coddle the dog or try to comfort him when he's afraid. This will only let the dog know that he has a reason to be worried and it will encourage him to be fearful the next time he experiences something new. Instead, remain calm, quiet, and confident. Dogs are experts at body language and they'll understand that there's no reason to be concerned. If you find yourself struggling to correct this type of behavior, don't hesitate to contact a professional trainer. The sooner you can get help, the less likely it is that the behavior will escalate.

Digging

A dog who develops a habit of digging is not only a danger to your landscaping, but also to himself. The unsightly holes all over your yard may eventually result in him digging his way out of the yard. He may also damage his nails or paw pads digging through hard soil. Some dogs who dig may also end up ingesting small amounts of soil or various objects they find underground, resulting in digestive problems and potential intestinal blockages.

Photo Courtesy of Makenzie Burk

Some owners allow their dogs to embrace their love of digging. Rather than discourage the behavior, they try to redirect the dogs to dig in an appropriate place. Instead of digging up the flower bed, owners may set up a sand box or a fenced-off area containing soft soil where the dog can dig as he pleases, without the risk of injury or escape. If you would prefer your Poodle didn't dig up any part of your yard or garden, discouraging the behavior is relatively easy, but constant supervision and consistency are essential. Never let your dog roam the yard without supervision until you are confident he has dropped his bad habit.

As with aggressive behavior, when you see your dog start to dig, a sharp "No!" or a clap or stomp should be enough to surprise and distract your dog. As long as you are consistent in your corrections, your dog should eventually get tired of being startled every time he tries to dig and move on to other activities. If you have a particularly large yard, it may also be worth your while to invest in a louder correction in case your Poodle wanders far enough that your correction becomes less effective. Many pet stores sell whistles or small air horns that are loud enough to surprise your dog from any distance. If you have close neighbors, they may not appreciate your training tactics, so you may need to just keep your dog close enough to you to be corrected without tools. A long leash or tracking lead is a great way to give your dog enough freedom to explore without being able to get too far away from you.

Separation Anxiety

"Poodles can display a sign of jealousy if they aren't getting enough attention or feel a lack of it. They need the feel of love, because this breed is all about pleasing their owner."

Sharon Hoffman
Hofman's Toys

You must be mindful of the way you greet and say goodbye to your dog to prevent separation anxiety. It can be difficult and frustrating to curb this type of behavior. Dogs who exhibit separation anxiety typically whine, bark, or howl when left alone. They may also become destructive and chew up things around the house or soil their kennels or on the floor. In extreme cases, they may even try to escape their crate, house, or yard. It's easy to imagine how harmful these behaviors can become. Your neighbors certainly won't appreciate listening to your dog bark while you're away from home, nor will you appreciate coming home to a mess after a long day at work. It can also be dangerous for your dog, who may injure himself as his behavior escalates. In some cases, a professional trainer may need to be called to help the situation.

The first step in preventing separation anxiety, as well as fixing it, is to remain calm when leaving or entering the house. It can be difficult not to join your dog in excitement when you're reunited, but for your dog's well-being, you must remain calm. If you get excited when you come home or give him long, drawn-out goodbyes, you're just confirming that there's a reason for your dog to act out. This doesn't mean that you can't show your dog affection, but you must wait until after he's calmed down. After coming inside, take your time putting your things away and by the time you're done, your Poodle will likely be calm enough that you can pet him and say hello. Practice entering and leaving the house for a few seconds or minutes at a time, each time ignoring your dog completely. Your dog may become anxious the first few times you do this, but eventually, he should understand that you're coming right back and there's no reason to become excited. As his training progresses, you can leave him for longer periods of time and his level of anxiety should lessen as he understands that he's not being abandoned.

Running Away

No matter which size Poodle you bring home, running away is an incredibly dangerous habit for your dog to develop. Dogs may bolt out an open front door and potentially run into the street. Smaller Poodles may also become prey for wild animals or stray dogs. The world is a dangerous place for an unaccompanied puppy, so it's essential that you put in the time and effort to teach him a solid recall.

HELPFUL TIP
Pet Insurance

Pet insurance can help you cover the cost of unexpected vet bills, but it doesn't cover preexisting conditions, and there is usually a waiting period before coverage takes effect. That means you need to plan ahead and invest in pet insurance as soon as you bring your Poodle puppy home, before it has a costly emergency.

It's good practice to ask your dog to sit and wait politely before walking through any doorway. A dog who pushes past humans to get through the door first is disrespectful and must be taught that humans always go through first. It can be helpful to keep a short leash on your Poodle as he wanders through the house. This will allow you to grab him if he tries to squeeze out an open door or simply won't listen to you. Some owners also opt to stick a few treats in their pockets and occasionally call the dog to them. By practicing your dog's recall at random times and rewarding him with a delicious treat, you are reinforcing the desired behavior. You can also reward your dog for waiting politely at doorways. For outdoor practice, invest in a tracking lead, which is just a long nylon or leather leash. This allows you to give your dog some freedom outside, but will not allow him to run away if he tries to do so.

Bedtime

The most important aspect of developing a bedtime routine is consistency. If possible, try to do the same things every night at about the same time. The sooner your puppy understands the routine, the sooner he will calm down and sleep more quietly through the night. You must also decide where your Poodle will sleep and commit to that decision. Whether you ask him to sleep in a crate in your bedroom, or in his own space in another part of the house, you need to stand by your decision no matter how much he protests in the beginning. After several nights of a regular routine, he'll begin to understand what is expected of him and he should settle down quickly.

In order to encourage your puppy to get ready to for bed and sleep quietly, try to discourage him from any roughhousing or exuberant play before bed. Make sure the focus of his nighttime walks is going to the bathroom, not exploring or playing. The calmer you can keep him before bed, the more likely he is to go quietly to bed. Ideally, you should exercise him enough earlier in the day so that he is tired and ready to sleep.

In the beginning, you will probably be taking your puppy out for bathroom breaks throughout the night, but developing a regular food and potty break schedule can help reduce the frequency of his nocturnal outings. Be sure to feed him dinner early enough that he can begin to digest his food and take his post-dinner bathroom break well before bedtime. If you choose to free-feed your Poodle, pick up his food dish a few hours before bed to limit his intake. Most dogs will need to go outside soon after meals, so if you can develop a regular feeding routine, you can begin to predict when and how often your dog will need to go out. Limiting your dog's water intake before bed can also help your dog sleep longer through the night. As with food, picking up your puppy's water dish an hour or two before bed may discourage him from asking to go out during the night as frequently. No matter what your bedtime routine is, the final task before bed should always be a trip outside. The later you can take your puppy out, the longer you'll be able to sleep before he needs to go out again.

Photo Courtesy of Rachael Mavroudis.

Leaving Your Poodle Home Alone

During the first few months after bringing your Poodle home, it's not recommended to allow him to have access to the entire house. Allowing your dog too much freedom will only result in soiled floors and chewed-up personal items. It can be incredibly difficult to house-train a dog that is allowed to eliminate wherever he pleases when no one is home. By keeping your dog contained in his designated area or crate, you can discourage him from eliminating in the house and chewing on inappropriate items. You'll also be able to leave knowing he's safe and secure in his own space.

To encourage your dog to rest quietly while you're gone, try leaving him in his crate or secure area for short periods of time while you're home. Keeping him contained will help you accomplish household chores without being disturbed and he'll become more comfortable in his space without worrying that you've left him. This can help build his confidence and reduce the likelihood of him developing separation anxiety.

If you have any concerns about leaving your dog at home, you have a few options to give you peace of mind. First, there are many companies that make cameras specifically designed for pet owners. These cameras allow you to view your home on your computer or smartphone at any time while you're away. Some cameras even allow you to speak to your dog or toss him a treat. Another option is to hire a dog walker to check on your dog and take him out for a potty break during the workday. This may be the best option for owners who work long hours or those who don't want to leave their dog alone all day.

CHAPTER 6
House-Training

Different Options for House-Training

Depending on the size of Poodle you have adopted and your own preferences, you have several options for house-training your new dog. The most popular method is teaching your dog that the only appropriate place to eliminate is outdoors, sometimes in a specific location. This method requires consistency and dedication, but Poodles are intelligent dogs and learn new habits quickly. Another option is an indoor "potty patch" or litter box. This option works better for smaller dogs, such as Toy Poodles. Disposable puppy pads can also be used as either a long-term solution or just until your dog can be relied upon using one of the other methods.

If you choose to use the more traditional method of house-training, consistency is key. Some owners choose to take their dogs to the same location in their yard or neighborhood to help the dog understand what is expected of him. When taking your dog outside for a bathroom break, try to discourage him from playing or exploring the yard at first. After he goes to the bathroom, he can be praised and allowed to play and explore as much as you let him. This freedom also works as positive reinforcement and will encourage him to repeat the behavior in the future.

Indoor options for house-training work best with small dogs, simply because of the size of their messes. Bigger dogs, such as Standard Poodles, can easily be litter-box trained, but you would need quite a large litter box. This is also a great option for owners who live in extremely hot or cold climates, or for those who work long hours

HELPFUL TIP
Crate Training

Many people cringe at the thought of leaving their dog in a crate, but it's important to think about the future. There may come a time when your Poodle must be in a crate, like during a grooming appointment, at the vet, or in a boarding facility. Each of those situations can be stressful enough alone, but your dog's stress will only be increased if it is unused to spending time in a crate. Crate training your Poodle puppy will help prevent stress for it in the future, while also helping you with house-training.

and want their dogs to be able to relieve themselves as they please. Whether you choose a litter box, potty patch, or disposable puppy pads, make sure to set them up in a specific area and do not move them. Your dog will develop a routine much quicker if he can eliminate in the same location every time. As with outdoor house-training, a verbal cue and plenty of positive reinforcement will help your dog learn the desired behavior.

No matter which method of house-training you decide to use, you must be consistent in your supervision and routine. Never let your Poodle wander through the house unsupervised. Every time he is allowed to eliminate inside the house without correction is a setback in his training. However, if you do not catch him in the act, you cannot correct him. According to Bob and Penny Daugherty of Sundance Poodles, "If you don't catch them in the act, don't waste your time. Clean it up and go on your merry way." Your Poodle will not understand that he is being punished for his actions in the past.

The First Few Weeks

"A good rule of thumb is: puppies need to go potty every hour per month of life during the day. A two month old puppy will need to be let out every two hours; a six month old puppy needs to go out every six hours."

Terri L Creech
Bear Cove Standard Poodles

You will likely have to clean up more than a few messes during your first few weeks with your new Poodle. However, being as diligent and consistent as possible will help your puppy understand the rules of the house more quickly. According to Sherri Regalbuto of Just Dogs with Sherri, "When a puppy has an accident it is our fault, not theirs." The younger the puppy, the more frequently he will need to go to the bathroom. A good rule of thumb is that for every month of your dog's age, he can go one hour between potty breaks. This means a two-month-old puppy will need to go out every two hours and a six-month-old puppy will need to go out roughly every six hours. Unfortunately, this rule applies around the clock, so if you have a particularly young puppy, you will likely be getting out of bed several times during the night. Just remember, the more consistent you are in your training, the more quickly your dog will become house-trained.

During the first few weeks, or even months, after bringing your puppy home, remember to keep your expectations relatively low. You may forget to take him out on occasion and you will need to clean up a few messes. No one is perfect, and mistakes will be made. Stay positive and patient with your puppy and he will be house-trained before you know it. If you set your expectations too high, you will likely become disappointed and frustrated with your puppy's progress, which will only serve to upset him and set your training back even more.

Since accidents are inevitable, it's important to have the right supplies on hand for cleanup. Disposable, absorbent puppy pads make clean up a breeze. As long as your puppy does not try to chew on them or eat them, they can be laid out across his pen or crate and thrown in the trash once they're soiled. Setting your puppy's area up in a place with easy to clean floors can also help. It's much easier to wipe up a mess on tile or hardwood flooring than on a shag rug. Your local pet store or favorite online retailer likely has a variety of cleaning products that can help eliminate stains and odor. Since dogs are creatures of habit, some cleaners even contain certain enzymes to help clean the mess more thoroughly and discourage your dog from eliminating in the same area again.

Photo Courtesy of
Adélaïde Guillemaud

Positive Reinforcement

One of the most popular and successful methods of dog training is positive reinforcement. This simply means that when your dog performs a desired behavior, you reward him immediately afterward with treats, praise, play, or a marker such as a clicker. As his training progresses, you can reduce the intensity and frequency of his rewards, but in the beginning you want to lavish him with affection, give him only high-value treats, and play with his favorite toys. It's okay to make a big deal out of his good behavior at this stage. If he sees that his behavior gets more of a positive reaction from you, he's more likely to repeat that behavior in the future.

Initially, when you take your dog outside for a potty break, he's not going to be able to connect any verbal cue with the desired behavior. During the first stages of potty training, wait until you notice him getting ready to eliminate before giving him your chosen verbal cue. He may sniff, slow his pace, or walk in circles, so keep an eye on his body language. You can repeat the verbal cue a few times while he's going, to strengthen his connection between your words and his behavior. It's best to wait to praise him until he's finished. If your praise is particularly exciting, he may get distracted and stop what he's doing, so let him finish before pulling out the treats. Once he's done, feel free to praise and pet him, give him his favorite treat, or play a game with his favorite toy.

You will likely see the most progress in your dog's training using positive reinforcement, but you may also need to use negative reinforcement on occasion, namely when you catch him eliminating inside your home or in an inappropriate place. If you catch your Poodle in the act, use a sharp "No!", or a loud clap or stomp to startle him. If he stops what he's doing, simply pick him up and take him outside to finish. Be sure to reward him when he goes outside. Never hit or yell at your dog; it will only cause him to be afraid of eliminating in your presence. If you find that your dog has had an accident in the house, but you didn't see it happen, it's best to simply clean it up and move on. If you punish your dog after the fact, or rub his nose in it, he won't understand what you're trying to tell him, and it won't further his training. The more diligent you are about supervising your puppy and taking him out at regular intervals, the less likely it is that you will find messes around your house.

Photo Courtesy of
Sherri-Ann Harris

Crate Training

One of the most helpful tools in house-training that any dog owner can use is the crate. Some owners may balk at the idea of keeping their beloved Poodle in a crate while they're away from the house or unable to supervise their dog, but it's important to remember that dogs are not humans. While you may not find comfort in a cozy, enclosed space, your dog thinks differently. With proper training, dogs learn to enjoy their time in the crate and will readily go inside without prompting. You may even find that your dog prefers to sleep inside his crate even when the crate door is left open and he is free to roam. Most dogs will not choose to eliminate in the same area that they sleep, so by confining your Poodle to a smaller space, he is less likely to make a mess before you are able to take him for his next potty break.

If your dog has never been in a crate before, or becomes anxious or nervous when put in one, you may need to introduce the crate slowly. You want to make him understand that the crate is not a punishment, it's a comfortable place where he can enjoy a little peace and quiet. If he's not a chewer, place a few cozy blankets, towels, or a dog bed inside. If you can take him outside for a walk or have a long play session before asking him to stay in the crate, he may be more inclined to relax and take a nap rather than become distressed. Introduce the crate by tossing a few treats in and verbally praising him when he enters. Eventually, you can begin closing the door behind him and allow him to stay inside for a few seconds at a time. As his training progresses, you can practice crating him while you do housework or relax at home. He'll learn quickly that the crate is a comfortable place that he can retreat to when he feels overwhelmed.

Be careful about what you put in your Poodle's crate while he's unattended. A puppy who chews can easily rip pieces off blankets, beds, or toys if given enough time. He could easily swallow these pieces and choke or develop an intestinal blockage. If you notice your puppy chewing on things, either remove them or supervise him while he has the item. It's not recommended to leave food and water in your puppy's crate while you're away either. Even if the bowls are attached to the sides of the crate, he is likely to spill them and soil his bedding, forcing him to sit on wet blankets until you return. He will also be more likely to urinate or defecate in his crate if he has access to food and water all day. Don't worry, he won't suffer without food and water for a few hours at a time, but be sure to give him access to clean, fresh water as soon as you release him from the crate.

Playpens and Doggy Doors

Once your dog has progressed with his house-training and he can be trusted to hold it for longer periods of time, you may want to consider investing in either a playpen or doggy door. Neither option is appropriate for dogs who have just begun house-training, since it allows the dog too much freedom, but once the dog has a basic understanding of house-training, he

Photo Courtesy of
Ellen Gettenberg

can be given a bit more space to roam. Playpens are a great intermediate step, as they allow the dog more freedom than a crate, but he is not yet given unrestricted access to the entire house. If you trust your Poodle not to get into trouble in your absence but want him to be able to relieve himself as needed, your next step can be installing a doggy door.

There are many types of playpens available on the market depending on your own personal preferences. The most inexpensive varieties are made of wire or plastic. They are typically made up of four or more panels and can be moved to fit whatever shape you feel is necessary for your dog's space. More expensive playpens are usually made of wood or clear acrylic or plastic. Use your best judgment to decide which material you like best and what size and height is most appropriate for your dog. Bigger Poodles will need taller playpens while smaller Poodles may do fine with shorter panels. If your dog is a jumper, you may need to look for a covered playpen to contain him.

If you're interested in a doggy door, you have a few options. If you have a sliding glass patio door, you may be interested in the type of removable door that can be placed in the door frame. With this type of doggy door, you will be sacrificing the use of your patio door, but they are generally less expensive and less invasive than a permanent doggy door. Permanent doggy doors can either be installed in your back door or through one of your exterior walls. Typically, the latter have more depth than removable doors or those that are installed in wooden or metal doors, as they must go through the width of your house's wall. They often have two flaps to help insulate the door and prevent drafts inside your home. With some encouragement and plenty of positive reinforcement, your Poodle will quickly learn how to go in and out of his new doggy door.

Be aware, however, that if you choose to install a doggy door, you may be leaving your home open to invasion if you aren't careful. If you own smaller dogs, such as Toy Poodles, the doors will be too small for a human to fit through, but a human could easily fit through a Standard-Poodle-sized doorway. Similarly, wild animals such as raccoons or skunks, or even other neighborhood pets or strays can easily enter your home through a doggy door. The easiest way to prevent an unwanted visitor is to close and lock the door while you aren't home. There are also doors that remain locked unless your dog approaches with a specific tag on his collar, allowing him to enter or exit. If an animal without a tag approaches, the door will remain locked.

You should also be cautious about allowing your dog unsupervised access to the yard while you're away from home. Toy Poodles and even Miniature Poodles are small enough that they can easily be snatched by neighborhood coyotes or birds of prey. Poodles of any size may also be able to dig under or jump over your fence and escape. Depending on the security of your yard, your dog could also be let out or stolen by neighbors or strangers. There is also the risk of him ingesting something dangerous that he finds in the yard. Before you allow your dog to use the doggy door while you're gone, consider how responsible he is in your absence and whether or not it's safe to allow him to go outside without supervision.

CHAPTER 7
Socializing with People and Animals

"Socializing is extremely important. That said you can over socialize and do more damage than good. Each poodle is an individual so it is important for new guardians to get to know their poodle quickly. Having friends with 'puppy friendly' dogs come over to interact is the best way to socialize with other dogs."

Sherri Regalbuto
Just dogs with Sherri

Importance of Good Socialization

If you plan on traveling with your dog, or you regularly have friends and family visit your home, you will expect your Poodle to be on his best behavior. Good socialization is an essential part of any dog's training program. Properly socialized Poodles are an absolute joy to be around. They are confident, friendly ambassadors of the breed. Well-socialized dogs are welcomed in dog-friendly public spaces and hotels, so no matter where you choose to bring your dog, he will leave a positive impression on people.

Traveling with dogs can be difficult, especially if your dog isn't socialized very well. A nervous, insecure dog who barks at strangers is unlikely to be welcomed in most hotels and public areas. If you plan on flying with your Poodle or traveling by train or bus, your trip may end in disaster if you do not properly prepare your dog for the experience.

It's also important to properly socialize your Poodle because it allows your dog to have the best life possible. An insecure, unsocialized dog will not enjoy walks around the neighborhood, visits to the park, or the company of friends and family. These experiences will put a significant amount of stress on your dog and he may react badly, either by trying to escape the situation or by lashing out. Having to manage an anxious dog will also put a lot of stress and responsibility on you as an owner. You will constantly have to worry about how your dog is going to react to new environments and situations. To prevent you and your dog from being overwhelmed by new people, places, and animals, it's best to start socializing as soon as possible. Once your Poodle receives all of his core vaccines, you can begin exposing him to new situations.

Behavior Around Other Dogs

Before you introduce your Poodle to other dogs, it's important to have a basic understanding of canine body language. A wagging tail does not always mean the dog is happy, and if you miss important cues, you may end up breaking up a fight rather than preventing it from happening in the first place. Dogs who greet each other in a friendly manner generally approach each other in a relaxed manner with tails wagging, alert ears, and a relaxed head position. If you notice any stiffening of the body, raising of the head or hackles, be cautious about continuing the introduction. Dogs who are fearful may also cower, urinate, or lick their lips submissively. This can sometimes trigger a reaction from a more aggressive dog, so keep a close eye on all dogs involved and if you have any doubts, remove your dog from the situation immediately.

When introducing your dog to others, it's best to do so on neutral territory. If you're bringing your Poodle home to meet your other pets, or are introducing him to your friends' dogs, try to do so out of their normal territory. With unvaccinated or under-vaccinated puppies, use caution when deciding where to set up the meeting. Often, the front yard, garage, or even a room that the dogs don't use often, such as a laundry room or dining room, can work as a neutral space. It's also

Photo Courtesy of Connie Hucks

Photo Courtesy of Charlotte Haugen Ladegård

best to restrain all dogs involved in case anything should happen. If the dogs are allowed to meet freely and a fight breaks out, it can be more difficult to separate them, and you are at risk of being bitten if you try to intervene. If the dogs are wearing leashes, it's much easier to separate them. Be aware, however, that if there is tension between the dogs, it's not uncommon for a fight to break out between them once the additional pressure of a leash is applied.

It's also essential that you remain calm and relaxed during any introduction with strange dogs. Your Poodle will be looking to you for guidance and if you show signs of anxiety or nervousness, he will pick up on that and is likely to be insecure as well. Even if you are nervous, try to relax and hold the leash loosely. Try not to tense up, and pretend to be confident if you must. If your dog senses that you aren't worried about a situation, he is more likely to approach the other dogs in a friendly, relaxed manner. Remember, dogs are social animals and they love playing, so be confident in your dog's ability to greet others properly and make new friends.

Ways to Socialize Your Poodle with Other Pets

"I advise new owners not to take their puppy to dog parks or around other dogs until they are completely vaccinated. Then they can slowly introduce them by letting them sniff of each other while keeping them on a leash. That way the owner always has control of the pet."

Sharon Hoffman
Hofman's Toys

If you have pets other than dogs at home, it's important to consider that this may be the first time your new Poodle has ever met an animal of that species. It might be overwhelming to both your new puppy and your other pet, so take things slowly. Your pets may not get along right away and that's okay, so be prepared for them to take some time to get along. You may need regular introductions over a period of weeks or months before the animals can be trusted together. Be patient, calm, and never rush the introductory period. Not all species have similar body language and it can take a while before they understand they are not a threat to each other.

Photo Courtesy of Susan Ruderman

As with dogs, it may be helpful to have the other pet meet the dog outside of their normal territory. Sometimes, this isn't possible or necessary, so use your best judgment according to the species you're introducing to your puppy. Wherever you choose to introduce the animals, make sure each pet is restrained, especially if there is a significant size difference between them. Whether you are introducing your Toy Poodle to your pet bird, or your Standard Poodle puppy to your cat, make sure everyone's safety is a priority. It's also necessary to be aware of each animal's body language. If either pet seems uncomfortable at any time, separate them immediately and try again later. This can be an overwhelming and stressful experience and you don't want to leave a negative impression on them. As with introductions with other dogs, it's important to remain calm and confident yourself. Your dog and your other pets will likely sense any tension or anxiety from you and they may react accordingly, so take a deep breath and try not to be nervous.

Never leave your Poodle puppy unsupervised with another animal until you are completely certain they can be trusted together. Accidents can happen in the blink of an eye, so make sure you are confident both your Poodle and the other pet can behave responsibly. In some cases, it may even be necessary to supervise their time together long-term. Toy Poodles, for instance, can be severely injured or even killed by larger pets, so it may be in your puppy's best interest to either keep them separated or only allow them to interact under close supervision. This advice also applies to small pets such as rabbits, birds, rodents, and even cats. Some Poodles have high prey drives and they may try to chase or kill a little animal. You will know your pets better than anyone, so use your best judgment to determine when or if they can ever be left alone together.

Properly Greeting New People

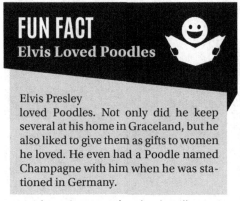

One of the most important aspects of socialization is introducing your Poodle to new people. This can be done both at home and around your neighborhood or city. Meeting as many different types of people as possible will help your Poodle gain the confidence to act responsibly while in public. Some puppies may react to strangers in a fearful manner, while others may react with excitement, but both will require patience and training in order to become well-behaved, respectful adult dogs. The best place to start introducing other people is in your own home. Your puppy will feel comfortable in familiar surroundings and is less likely to react out of fear. As his training progresses, you'll be able to begin introducing him to your neighbors and eventually take him to the veterinarian, groomer, park, or shopping center.

As you begin introducing your puppy to new people, you need to remember to take it slowly, so your puppy doesn't become overwhelmed. Try introducing just one or two new people at a time and avoid crowds until he's a bit more confident. You should also discuss your socialization goals with new people before allowing them to meet your puppy. Explain to them how he typically reacts to new people and how you would prefer that he react. If he tends to jump excitedly onto people's laps, tell them the puppy must sit quietly before they are allowed to touch him. If he tends to be fearful, warn them that he may cower or try to avoid them and that they shouldn't try to grab him or make any quick movements. Remember not to coddle a fearful dog, as this will only make the behavior worse. Instead, be positive and encouraging and reward even small steps toward new people. The ideal reaction is a calm dog that greets people politely, without intruding into their space or jumping on them.

Using positive reinforcement will help your puppy learn the correct way to greet people. After explaining your expectations to the new people, it may be helpful to give them a few treats and ask them to reward your puppy when he behaves properly. Fearful puppies may be coaxed toward strangers with treats, and rambunctious puppies can be rewarded for sitting patiently. Although petting often works as a reward in itself, puppies will often learn more quickly when their favorite food is involved.

Poodles and Children

Poodles' intelligence and gentle, friendly nature make them excellent companions for children. With proper introductions and supervision, your Poodle and your children can become best friends. It can be a wonderful experience for a child to grow up with the companionship of a Poodle, but it does take preparation and training. Dogs and children must both be prepared for the experience and taught proper manners. If adequate training and supervision do not take place, it can be a dangerous situation for both the dog and the child. An overly enthusiastic child can easily injure a delicate puppy, especially smaller dogs such as Toy Poodles. Likewise, an excited or scared puppy may bite and seriously hurt a child. However, these tragedies are easily prevented as long as you are willing to put the time and effort into your dog's training.

Before introducing your new Poodle to your children, it can be helpful to sit with them and have a discussion about proper behavior around animals. In their excitement over meeting their new family member, the kids may have difficulty focusing on your instructions, so explaining everything beforehand can help prepare them. Explain to them how to gently pet a puppy and how they can avoid frightening the puppy. If they are especially young children, try to discourage them from picking the puppy up, as even a short fall can injure a delicate young puppy. You may also want to discuss their role in the puppy's care, if they have one. This can be a great opportunity to teach children about responsibility. Most importantly, you must explain to the kids that they are not to interact with the puppy without adult supervision.

In the beginning, you may need to keep your puppy separated from your children except when you can carefully supervise the situation. Setting your puppy's private space up in an area of your home where your children spend a lot of time can help him adjust to life with rambunctious kids. Having a secluded area that he can retreat to away from the kids, such as a crate or bed, will allow him a place to take a break should he feel overwhelmed. It's also important to take these introductions slowly. As with introductions to other animals, it's important to keep an eye on both the children and the puppy, and if you notice anyone showing signs of discomfort or anxiety, separate them immediately. You may only be able to allow them to interact for a few moments at a time at first, but over time they will adjust to each other's presence and they'll be able to play together for longer periods of time. No matter what, you should never leave children unattended with a puppy. Accidents can happen quickly and it's essential that you are there to prevent them.

CHAPTER 8

Poodles and Your Other Pets

Introducing Your New Puppy to Other Animals

The most important aspect of introducing your new Poodle puppy to other animals is to respect each animal's boundaries. Some animals may be perfectly comfortable with a bouncy, exuberant puppy, while others may become fearful or irritable. Likewise, your puppy may not be entirely comfortable getting too close to certain animals. Careful supervision and a basic knowledge of body language can help prevent any unnecessary accidents.

As with any other introduction, approach the situation slowly but calmly and with confidence. Most animals are experts in body language and will be able to tell if you are acting nervously. This will cause them to approach the introduction with anxiety, increasing the chances of a negative experi-

Photo Courtesy of Betsy Johnson

ence. Depending on the type of animal you are introducing your Poodle to, you may need to keep your puppy at a comfortable distance at first. Certain prey animals, such as sheep or horses, react to dogs as if they are predators, so until they realize the dog is not a threat, they may need a little extra space. Dogs can also become uncomfortable around especially large animals, such as horses or cattle, so only allow the animals to be as close as they are comfortable. Restraint is also an important aspect of a proper introduction. This will allow you to remove each animal from the situation quickly and easily should something go wrong. If you are introducing your Poodle to livestock, this may be as simple as keeping your dog on a leash and the other animals behind a fence.

As your Poodle becomes more comfortable around other animals, and vice versa, you can make the decision whether to allow the animals to interact freely, without restraint. In some situations, this may never be a good idea, but it's up to you to decide. Toy and Miniature Poodles are quite small and can be stepped on by an angry or unaware horse, so allowing your puppy to roam freely in the stable may not be the best idea. Poodles with high prey drives may also find it difficult to interact with poultry without chasing or attacking. As you work with your puppy, you'll get a better idea of his personality and will be better able to predict his behavior in certain situations. You should also have some idea of how the other animals will react to your Poodle after they get used to him, so use your best judgment to decide when and how they will be allowed to interact with each other.

Pack Mentality

It may be difficult to look at your Poodle and believe he is the descendant of wolves, but his behavior in regard to his pack definitely reflects his wild heritage. Dogs, like wolves, are social animals and conduct themselves according to a strict hierarchy in their group. Dogs are most comfortable as followers but will take over the position as leader if they are not provided with proper boundaries and guidance. Some dogs are naturally more submissive then others and will fall into line much more easily. More dominant dogs may constantly challenge the leader and may need more work to keep them in place. It's important to be aware that this hierarchy is dependent on a dog's individual personality, rather than size. A Toy Poodle is just as likely to challenge you as his pack leader as a Standard Poodle. Whether you have an entire pack of dogs or other pets, or just a single Poodle, it's important that you set clear boundaries and maintain your position as leader of the pack. A dog of any size without rules and limitations can easily become unmanageable or even dangerous.

For small dogs, such as Toy and Miniature Poodles, it's even more important to make sure that they understand their place in the pack hierarchy. Little dogs are often allowed to get away with more inappropriate behavior because they aren't considered to be as dangerous as larger dogs. This type of behavior is often referred to as 'small dog syndrome' and can be a challenge to correct if it isn't prevented. Behaviors such as resource guarding, jumping on people, refusing to obey commands, and being overly protective of his owner should be corrected each and every time your dog attempts them. This type of attitude is rarely tolerated in large dogs, but since small dogs are generally viewed as cute little stuffed animals rather than the descendants of wolves, they tend to get away with more bad behavior. If your Poodle starts to exhibit any of these behaviors, it needs to be corrected immediately to prevent it from escalating. If you are having trouble recognizing or correcting behaviors associated with small dog syndrome, contact a professional trainer or behavior specialist as soon as possible.

In natural pack settings, the leader of the pack is allowed to do as he pleases. He is the first to eat and can sleep wherever he wants. He never moves out of the way of other pack members and puts others in their place with growling, snapping, or showing his teeth. As the leader of your pack, it's essential that you act appropriately. If your Poodle is sitting in your favorite chair or in your spot in the bed, you must be willing to do what it takes to move him out of the way. When you feed your dog, try asking him to sit and wait politely, rather than diving into the bowl immediately. You must also be the first to walk through doorways and not allow your dog to shove his way past you. If you must correct your dog, never hit, yell, or kick your dog. This will only frighten your dog and will not establish your position as leader. Remaining calm, assertive, and consistent in your leadership will help you maintain a stable and manageable pack.

Fighting/Bad Behavior

If your puppy begins to exhibit any aggressive or inappropriate behavior, it's essential that you correct it immediately. If your corrections are inconsistent or nonexistent, this behavior will likely escalate, potentially leading to a fight. Your puppy must understand that this behavior will not be tolerated. This also applies to any other dogs already in your household. Older dogs should be allowed to correct an overly exuberant puppy, but they should never act aggressively. Terri L. Creech of Bear Cove Standard Poodles explains, "Understand that the puppy is coming into a home with pets that have been there for a while. An older dog may not want to be pestered by a puppy. They will correct the puppy, and as long as the older pets doesn't hurt the puppy, they are acting within their rights. Make sure they can get away from an annoying 'little brother' and have some quiet time alone." During the first few weeks or months after bringing your puppy home, it's important to supervise your pets during all interactions to make sure they are behaving themselves and that you can correct them if they are not.

Once your dog has begun to exhibit aggressive behavior, it's important to properly manage him and his surroundings to help prevent him from getting into a fight. In combination with proper training, his bad behavior may eventually disappear, but it will take time and effort to accomplish this. If you know your dog is a resource guarder, try to avoid situations in which he may feel the need to protect his possessions until you have better control over his behavior. You may want to remove toys from the house or feed the dogs in their own crates. If you cannot seem to get control over your dog's aggressive behavior, or have doubts about your abilities to do so, contact a professional trainer immediately. The sooner you get help, the better, because aggression will likely escalate over time and may result in tragedy.

If your dog does end up in a fight, take care in breaking up the fight to prevent yourself from being bitten. Never grab a dog by the collar as he can easily turn around and bite you. Even a dog who is not usually aggressive toward humans can bite during times of stress and extreme emotion. This is one of the only times that yelling at your dog is appropriate. Loud noises such as yelling, banging food bowls, or stomping can help distract the dogs

Photo Courtesy of Nick and Krysta Ventriglio

and break up the fight. If you have water near you, throwing water on the dogs can also surprise them and end the fight. If you absolutely must physically intervene, try using an item such as a board, playpen panel, or even a blanket to separate the dogs. If you are still unable to separate the dogs, decide which dog is the aggressor and grab him by the back legs and pull him away from the other dog. You must do this quickly, however, so that he doesn't have the chance to turn around to bite you. Once you have the dogs separated, it's crucial that you restrain both dogs immediately to prevent another fight.

Aggressive behavior can be incredibly dangerous and difficult to correct, so you need to be willing to admit when you need help. If you have any doubts about your ability to handle an aggressive dog, you need to contact a professional trainer immediately. A trainer will not only help you learn techniques to correct aggressive behavior but will help you learn to manage your dog and his surroundings to prevent fights. Dog fights have serious consequences and must be taken seriously, so don't be afraid to seek help as soon as possible.

Raising Multiple Puppies from the Same Litter

Dogs are social animals and are generally happy to share their home with other dogs. It might be reasonable to assume that they would be even happier to grow up alongside one of their littermates. However, there are important factors to consider when deciding whether or not to bring home two or more puppies from the same litter. Not only will you be cleaning up more messes, but two puppies will cost you more money, though your puppy will have a constant companion, which may help in preventing separation anxiety. If you do decide to adopt multiple puppies, carefully consider whether or not you are willing and able to take on the extra work and responsibility.

Raising multiple puppies from the same litter can be a very rewarding experience. You'll be able to see them progress alongside each other in their training. You will need to take them for daily walks, of course, but having multiple dogs means more opportunities for them to exercise themselves. Puppies love to play, and multiple puppies are guaranteed to wear themselves out if allowed to play as much as they like. You will also worry less when leaving your dogs home alone, knowing that they have companions to keep them company until you return home. Additionally, adopting littermates solves the potentially complicated situation of introducing dogs who do not know each other.

Unfortunately, bringing home littermates also presents quite a few problems. Multiple puppies can get into trouble much faster and be more destructive if left unsupervised. You will also have to dedicate a significant amount of time to training multiple dogs. Each dog will need regular individual training sessions, so be prepared to spend more time working with your dogs. Dogs who are raised with littermates can also develop severe anxiety when separated if they aren't regularly allowed to be on their own. Taking your dogs on individual walks and leaving each of them home alone on a regular basis can help them gain the confidence to be on their own. House-training will also be significantly more difficult with more than one dog. You will need to supervise multiple dogs in the house and yard as well. You must also consider the financial burden of multiple dogs. You will be buying more food and paying for more veterinary care and grooming appointments. Raising littermates can be a rewarding experience, but you must decide whether you are ready for the commitment.

Options if Your Pets Don't Get Along

HELPFUL TIP
Poodles Prefer People

Poodles generally prefer the company of humans over that of other dogs. However, they are also predisposed to separation anxiety, boredom, and depression if left alone too long, so having another pet to keep your Poodle company when you're away can be a good thing.

When you're introducing your new Poodle puppy to your current dogs or other pets, don't be too concerned if they do not get along right away. Older pets may be set in their ways and resistant to change and may need extra time to adapt to living with a puppy. You may need to keep them separated for a few weeks or months until they get used to each other. It's essential that you remain calm and patient throughout this introductory phase and do not rush the natural progression of your pets' relationship. Some animals just need more time, but on occasion there may be pets that simply don't want to live together.

Giving up a beloved pet is a heartbreaking decision, so carefully consider whether this is the best option for your circumstances. Some owners love their pets dearly and are willing to manage their household in a way that limits the animals' interactions, rather than giving one of them away. Understand that keeping and managing two animals who don't get along is a lifelong responsibility, especially if their behavior toward each other is aggressive. It can be time consuming and exhausting to feed, exercise, and groom two or more pets that can't be trusted to be together. You will need to provide them with separate, comfortable accommodations where they cannot access each other. It can also be difficult to ensure that each animal is given enough attention and affection to keep it happy. It may be possible to work with a professional trainer who can help familiarize the animals over time.

Another option is to find a new home for one of your pets. This is a decision not to be taken lightly, but if it necessary for the animals' well-being, then it may be your best option. Some animals are happier as single pets, while others simply need a companion with a different temperament. If you've exhausted your other options and can see no way to manage your pets' dislike for each other for the next 10-15 years, it may be time to call it quits. It's a heartbreaking decision to have to make, but as a pet owner, your pets' well-being is your responsibility and you must do your best to ensure your pets' needs are being met to the best of your ability.

CHAPTER 9
Physical and Mental Exercise

"Poodles are as individually different as human beings. Some need to be walked two to three times a day or just be out in the yard where you can throw the ball and allow them to run or chase a Frisbee."

Sharon Heath
Kokopelli Standard Poodles

Exercise Requirements

No matter what size Poodle you decide to bring home, you should plan on spending at least 30 minutes per day exercising him. Most healthy, able-bodied dogs would prefer more than 30 minutes of strenuous exercise, so if you have the time they will gladly play or exercise with you for as long as possible. Obviously, older dogs with mobility issues and young puppies with growing bones and joints should be exercised less than healthy adult dogs. For dogs with physical health problems, you can focus more on mental stimulation to keep them happy and out of trouble. Poodles are incredibly intelligent dogs and if you don't find a way to keep their overactive minds busy, they will typically find their own activity, but it may not be something you approve of. No matter what type of exercise you decide to do with your Poodle, it's recommended to check with your veterinarian to see if your dog is healthy enough for that level of activity. Like humans, dogs typically need to build up their fitness and stamina, so go slowly and increase your dog's activity levels over a period of weeks or months. Young Poodles can suffer from permanent joint damage if they exercise too strenuously before the growth plates in their bones close, so go easy on your dog until he is around 12 to 18 months old.

According to Sherri Regalbuto of Just Dogs with Sherri, "Exercise is an important part of living with Poodles." Dogs who do not receive enough physical and mental stimulation may develop both health and behavior problems as a result of their inactivity and boredom. Dogs who do not exercise enough may gain weight, which can lead to obesity-related health

problems such as arthritis, diabetes, and heart and respiratory disease. Overweight dogs also typically have shorter life spans than dogs kept at a healthy weight. Poodles were bred to be active sporting dogs and as such, they do not do well with sedentary lifestyles. If you are an active person, your Poodle will gladly accompany you on long walks, hikes, or runs. They also very successful in most dog sports, so if you're looking to compete with your dog, the Poodle may be your ideal partner.

Ensuring your dog receives enough mental exercise is just as important as making sure he gets his physical exercise every day. All dogs need a certain amount of mental stimulation to prevent boredom-related bad habits, but this is especially important for highly intelligent breeds such as the Poodle. A bored Poodle is a destructive Poodle. A Poodle who doesn't receive enough daily mental stimulation may develop bad habits such as chewing, barking, escaping, or getting into the trash. The breed typically learns quickly and can be taught new tasks in a matter of minutes, so it's better to teach them desirable behaviors rather than let them teach themselves. Poodles thrive in obedience competitions and are often used as trick dogs, so if you're looking for a dog that you can constantly teach new commands to, your Poodle will be an eager student.

Photo Courtesy of Andrew Wood

Different Types of Exercise to Try

Poodles are versatile and athletic dogs, capable of succeeding in many different types of dog sports. However, they are also individuals with their own likes and dislikes. You may want to try different types of exercise to figure out what works best for you and your dog. Some sports require more physical activity on your part, while others require more from your dog. There are lower-impact sports for dogs with physical limitations and high-speed sports for dogs who need to burn off a lot of energy. Before you introduce your dog to any activity, find out what sport clubs exist in your area. You should be able to find a group who will allow you to come watch them practice or even compete. You can talk to other handlers and see if it is something you'd like to try with your own dog. You may even find other Poodle owners who can help with introducing your dog to this new sport. If you find that you or your dog aren't enjoying a particular activity, don't feel bad about quitting. There are so many different ways to exercise your dog, you don't need to spend time doing something you don't enjoy.

Obedience is a sport in which Poodles of all sizes can excel. Their incredible intelligence allows them to learn quickly, while their dedication to their owners and willingness to please make them focused and eager learners. In obedience, a dog is asked to perform a series of commands including heel, sit, down, and stay. There are different levels of competition and the challenge increases with each level. Lower levels are performed on-leash and only basic commands and short stays are required. More advanced levels of competition require the dog to perform off-leash and the stays are longer and the commands more complex.

If you're looking for something more fast-paced, try agility. Agility is a sport in which dogs must make their way through an obstacle course as quickly as possible. There are jumps, tunnels, weave poles, and more. Dogs are faulted if they miss an obstacle or knock down a jump pole. Jumps vary in height and are adjusted according to the size of the dog competing. Dogs only compete against others of similar size, so you won't find a Toy Poodle competing against a Standard Poodle.

Flyball is an exciting team sport where dogs take turns racing over a series of small hurdles before pouncing on a box that releases a tennis ball. Once the dog has the ball, he turns around and makes his way back over the hurdles to his handler. Once one dog has cleared the start line, the next dog can be released. The event is timed, and the fastest team wins. Poodles are excellent retrievers and particularly fast or energetic dogs may especially enjoy competing in flyball.

Dock diving is another sport that is perfect for Poodles. Although all breeds and sizes of dog may compete, water-loving retrievers such as the Poodle particularly enjoy taking part. This is not a timed sport, but rather a test of the dog's jumping ability. A toy is hung in front of a platform above a long, rectangular pool of water and the dog must jump out into the water to grab it. The dog who jumps the furthest distance wins.

If you're looking to get your exercise along with your dog, you may be interested in Canicross. This is a relatively new sport where a dog wears a harness similar to those fitted on sled dogs. The leash is attached to either a harness worn around your waist, or your bicycle. The dog then runs in front of you, either on your feet or on your bicycle. Canicross races vary in distance and terrain, but it's a great opportunity to bond with your Poodle through a physical challenge.

Photo Courtesy of Emil Friberg

Importance of Mental Exercise

Mental exercise is just as important as physical exercise. If your Poodle isn't given enough opportunities to work his mind, he'll likely find some on his own. Terri L. Creech of Bear Cove Standard Poodles says, "A naughty Poodle usually needs more exercise." If your Poodle becomes bored, he may try to entertain himself by chewing on furniture or personal items, digging in the yard, or getting into the trash can. Poodles' intelligence means

HELPFUL TIP
Poodles Need to Work

Despite their reputation as being "prissy," Poodles were bred to work all day. Standard Poodles were developed to retrieve ducks and other waterfowl for hunters, while Miniature Poodles were bred to sniff out truffles in the woods. Even though Toy Poodles were bred for companionship, they still have more energy than some other Toy Breeds thanks to their working ancestors.

they can be quite creative in the ways in which they entertain themselves. Unfortunately, this also means their ability to learn quickly applies to bad habits. If your dog figures out how to open the back gate once, he's likely to repeat the behavior. To prevent your Poodle from developing behavioral problems, it's important that you keep his mind busy. A tired dog is a well-behaved dog.

Dog sports are a great way to keep your dog exercised, both physically and mentally. Each sport has a certain level of mental stimulation which can be a great way to keep your dog out of trouble. If you don't plan on competing or would like to keep your dog busy in between practice sessions, you can simply work your dog's mind with regular training sessions. Depending on your dog's age and level of training, it's best to keep these sessions short. A dog can become surprisingly exhausted after a five to 15-minute training session. However, you want to quit before your dog completely loses focus on you. You can always give him a break and begin another short session later. Poodles are capable of learning an incredible variety of commands, so don't be afraid to get creative with your training.

You can also exercise your Poodle's mind with fun games and toys at home. There are many different toys on the market that require your dog to use his brain to figure them out. Most involve placing a small amount of food or a treat inside and the dog must think about what he must do to get it out. This may include nudging the toy, moving flaps or sliding pieces, or moving the toy with his paw. Toys are available in a variety of sizes and difficulty levels, so you should be able to find the perfect puzzle toy for your dog. Many owners choose to keep a few on hand and switch them out once in a while to prevent their dogs from becoming bored with just one toy.

Tips for Keeping Your Poodle Occupied

Poodle owners who work long hours are always looking for new ways to keep their dogs busy while they're away or just so they can get work done around the house. Your local pet store or favorite online retailer likely has a huge selection of puzzle toys and games to keep your dog busy. Since most dogs are food- motivated, most of the toys must be filled with treats or dog food. To prevent your dog from consuming too many extra calories while he exercises his brain, you may want to feed a portion of his daily meals in a puzzle toy. This can be an excellent way to motivate your dog to figure out the puzzle or toy without contributing to any weight gain.

During the warmer months, you may want to try freezing your dog's food-filled toys for an extra challenge and a refreshing treat. This can be a little messy, so if you're concerned about cleanup you can give your dog his frozen treat outside. If you usually use dry treats or kibble in your dog's toys, you can try mixing it with a little yogurt, baby food, or canned dog food before putting it in the freezer. Dogs who are usually able to get the food

Photo Courtesy of
Jasper Roam

out of their toys quickly may be kept busy for longer periods of time when their food is frozen. This is a great option for both young and old dogs since it keeps their mind active but doesn't put too much strain on their bodies.

Another food-filled option to keep your Poodle occupied is a snuffle mat. These mats can be homemade or store-bought and are typically made of a soft and washable material such as fleece. The snuffle mat is just a small rug with various flaps and strips of fabric covering its surface. Simply take a handful of treats or kibble and sprinkle it over the mat. You may need to ruffle the fabric around to properly bury the treats within the mat. Your dog then has to use his nose to search for the individual treats or pieces of kibble among the strips of fabric. Snuffle mats can get dirty quickly, so if you're making one yourself it's best to choose a fabric that can be easily washed.

Some Poodle owners take the concept of a snuffle mat and increase the challenge by hiding treats all over the house or room. This can only be done with dogs that are house-trained and can be trusted to have access to more space than just their kennel. By hiding treats in corners, under chairs, and just out of sight, your dog must use his nose to search for and find all of the hidden treats. When hiding the treats, you can try closing your dog in a separate room or out in the yard, so he doesn't see where you put the treats. This type of scavenger hunt allows the dog to use his primal hunting instincts in a way that exercises both his mind and body. It's also a great way to exercise older dogs since it doesn't require much more physical strain than just walking around the house.

CHAPTER 10
Training Your Poodle

"Poodles are very easy to train due to their intelligence. The time spent on training at an early age is priceless. I talk to my poodles just like they are children and use key words that they know and understand."

Bob and Penny Daugherty
Sundance Poodles

Clear Expectations

Photo Courtesy of Jessica Yost

When beginning your training program with your Poodle, it's important to have clear expectations of both your dog and yourself. Poodles are incredibly intelligent dogs, but your dog's training will only progress according to how much time you spend working with him. If you only train him once or twice a week, he will progress much more slowly than if you have daily training sessions. Training sessions don't need to be long, typically around 15-20 minutes each, but they do need to be frequent enough that each session is building on the last, rather than refreshing the dog's memory of what you have previously worked on.

During any training session, it's essential that you ask yourself if your dog is truly ready for the next step. Progressing too quickly in your dog's training will leave him confused and frustrated. He may also become less

focused and less cooperative in his lessons. For example, if you have recently taught your dog to stay and he is staying in position reliably in your living room, you shouldn't take him to a busy park and expect him to stay just as well as he does at home. He simply isn't ready for that big of a leap in his training. It can be frustrating if you aren't seeing progress as quickly as you'd like, but it's important that you take a deep breath and understand that each step is progress, no matter how small. Eventually, you will look back at your dog's training and you will be amazed at how far he has come.

If your dog seems to be struggling with a new concept and he's becoming tired and unfocused in his training session, you need to be sure to end the session on a good note. Ending a training session with a frustrated dog may leave a negative impression on him and he may be less enthusiastic about his next session. Instead, try going back to something he has already learned and can perform reliably. Just asking him to sit quietly a few times and rewarding him for it can put you both in a better mood and looking forward to the next training session.

Operant Conditioning Basics

One of the most well-known methods of learning, known as operant conditioning, is a process in which an individual learns tasks through a system of rewards and punishment. The American psychologist and behaviorist B.F. Skinner popularized this method during his studies in the 1930s. Skinner theorized that both animals and humans are complex creatures that are capable of learning through methods other than classical conditioning. He suggested that behaviors are more likely to be repeated if they are followed by a positive experience or the removal of a negative sensation and that behaviors are less likely to be repeated if followed by a negative experience. The environmental responses that encouraged the repetition of a behavior were referred to by Skinner as either positive or negative reinforcers. He also suggested that neutral reinforcers are environmental responses that have no impact on the likelihood of a behavior being repeated in the future. The negative responses to a behavior are called punishments and decrease the likelihood of the individual repeating the behavior.

In dog training, one of the most popular methods of training involves positive reinforcement. This reinforcement often comes in the form of praise or treats, but toys, playtime, and markers work well too. Poodles are intelligent dogs who love attention, so they typically learn quickly when positive reinforcement is used. Terri L. Creech of Bear Cove Standard Poodles says, "They really want to please and will do what you want just because it pleases you." Most dogs are also food-motivated, especially when their favorite treats are involved. Unfortunately, positive reinforcement can also encourage dogs to repeat undesirable behaviors. For example, if your Poodle dashes out the front door and is rewarded with an exciting romp around the neighborhood, he's more likely to repeat this behavior in the future. If he gets into the trash and finds a tasty snack, he's probably going to get into the trash again. Managing your dog's environment in a way that prevents him from getting to trouble is the best way to prevent bad behaviors. It's easier to prevent a behavior from developing than it is to correct it.

Negative reinforcement is not to be confused with punishment, as they are two very different aspects of the learning process. Negative reinforcement is when a behavior is encouraged by the removal of an unpleasant sensation. For example, if you are training your dog to sit using negative reinforcement, you may ask him to sit while gently pushing on his rear end with your hand. The moment he sits, the pressure is released. Although the pressure isn't causing him any pain, it's likely not very comfortable, so he learns quickly that he must sit in order to avoid that pressure on his rear. Negative reinforcement is best used in combination with positive reinforce-

*Photo Courtesy of
Connie Hucks*

ment to ensure that the dog understands what you're asking and is more likely to repeat that behavior in the future. If you use the previously mentioned method of asking your dog to sit and follow his correct behavior with either praise or a delicious treat, you have successfully used both positive and negative reinforcement.

Punishment differs from negative reinforcement because it is used to discourage a dog from repeating a behavior in the future. For example, if your dog begins digging a hole in the yard and you stomp, clap, or tell him "No!" every time he begins to dig, after a few attempts he will likely connect his digging behavior to the loud and unpleasant noises coming from you. He will understand that digging will be met with a negative response from you, so he will be less likely to repeat the behavior in the future. However, you must never be too harsh in the punishment you use in training. Rather than stop the behavior, your dog is more likely to become fearful towards you.

Primary Reinforcements – Food, Toys, Playtime

The main type of rewards you will be using while training your dog are commonly referred to as primary reinforcements. These reinforcements are biological in nature and reward the dog on a primal level. Food is the most obvious biological reward in this category. Dogs need food to live and in the wild, their efforts at hunting are often rewarded with food when they finally catch their prey. Modern, domesticated dogs don't need to catch their own food, but they are capable of learning what behaviors they can perform to earn food from their owners. Toys and playtime are used less frequently in dog training, but they have the same effect on a dog. In the wild, dogs enjoy chasing and catching their prey, and this behavior can be simulated during playtime. Games like fetch and tug simulate behaviors that would be performed in the wild with prey. In some cases, toys and playtime may work better to motivate the dog, especially if they aren't particularly motivated by food or have a high prey drive.

Using food as a reward is one of the easiest ways to focus your dog's attention and keep him interested in the work. Some Poodles are highly motivated by food, while others may need some encouragement. For some dogs, any type of food will work. Food-motivated dogs will work just as hard for a piece of kibble as they will a piece of meat. These dogs tend to be easy to train simply because they will do anything for food. Training dogs who are not motivated by food can be a bit more difficult. You may need to try a few different types of treats to see what they are willing to work for.

*Photo Courtesy of
Sherie Jackson*

High-value treats such as meat, small pieces of cheese, or dehydrated liver often work well. Use these treats only while training to help the dog understand that he must work for these particularly delicious snacks.

If your Poodle is not motivated by food or has an especially high prey drive, you may want to try using a toy or playtime as your primary reinforcer. Typically, trainers who use toys as a reward use tugs, rubber balls, or toys attached to a rope. The reward system works exactly as it does with treats. When your dog performs the desired behavior, you can toss him the toy or let him grab it from the air. It can be helpful to move the toy away from the dog as you offer it. This forces him to chase the toy, if only for a moment, and makes the reward even more meaningful. Once he has the toy in his mouth, you can play tug with him or simply let him run around with his trophy. It may take some time to figure out the best toy for your individual dog and the best way of rewarding him with it, so don't be afraid to experiment during your initial training sessions.

Secondary Reinforcements – Attention, Praise, Clickers

Secondary reinforcements are a type of reward that must be taught to your dog. He won't automatically understand the value of "Good boy!" or the noise of a clicker until he begins to associate these responses with primary reinforcements. Many trainers choose to spend a few of their initial training sessions working on the dog's connection between primary and secondary reinforcements. For example, your first training session may consist of simply pressing the clicker or praising the dog as you hand him a treat. Eventually, he'll understand that the clicking sound or your chosen reward phrase means he'll receive food.

Attention and praise work well with Poodles as secondary reinforcements because Poodle love to please their owners. They love being lavished with attention, so there is a relatively short learning curve when using praise as a reward. However, it may help to choose a specific word or phrase to let your dog know that he's performed the correct behavior. Some owners choose words like "yes" or "good" to indicate that the dog has done well. There are trainers who also recommend different words for different expectations that you may have. You might choose to use one word to let the dog know he's doing the right thing, but that he's not done working yet, and a different word for when he is finished with that task. For instance, if you want the dog to sit and stay sitting while you praise him, you may want to use a specific word to let him know he's doing well but you'd like him to continue performing the behavior. You can use a different word to reward him when he's done well, and you are releasing him from that position. It will take some time and consistent conditioning for your dog to understand the difference, but eventually he will be able to tell when he's done working based on the verbal praise you give him.

Clickers also work well as secondary reinforcements, but it does take more time for the dog to associate the sound with good behavior. Initially, you will need to use classical conditioning to teach your dog the value of the clicker. You don't need to ask your dog to do anything; you simply press the clicker and hand him a treat. As you introduce this concept in training, he should eventually understand that the clicker means he's done a good job.

As you and your dog progress in his training, you may find it useful to limit your use of primary reinforcements. This will encourage your dog to work with you and perform the desired behaviors without you having to carry treats or his favorite toy in your pocket all the time. You'll be able to ask him to sit quietly while you drink coffee at a café or walk politely next to you down a busy street without worrying about how you're going to reward him. To keep your dog motivated, you may need to return to primary reinforcements once in a while, as the value of the secondary reinforcements may weaken over time.

Negative Reinforcement

Negative reinforcements are a commonly misunderstood aspect of dog training. As with many training tools, they can be extremely useful when used properly, but can cause harm if used incorrectly. Placing too much pressure on a dog with negative reinforcement can easily scare him and deter him from engaging with you in future training sessions. However, when properly combined with positive reinforcement, negative reinforcement can become a valuable tool in your training toolbox. For example, leash training can be much more effective when taught with negative reinforcement. Initially, when you put gentle pressure on the dog's leash, he may ignore you or even brace against the pressure. If he happens to step toward you, you immediately release the pressure and reward him with your chosen primary and secondary reinforcements. He will quickly learn that giving in to the leash pressure will not only result in the removal of that pressure, but he'll earn a treat as well.

You must be extremely careful when using negative reinforcement with your Poodle. They are an intelligent breed and can quickly learn both good and bad behaviors. You must keep an eye on your dog's body language at all times and practice perfect timing when releasing the pressure on your dog. If he performs the correct behavior and you do not immediately remove the negative sensation, the dog will not understand what you are asking of him. He may become confused and could develop aversive or fearful behaviors in future training sessions. While it is possible to train your dog using only negative reinforcements, he's more likely to enjoy the work and learn quicker when positive reinforcement is used as well.

Hiring a Trainer/Attending Classes

There are numerous benefits to hiring a trainer or attending obedience classes. Most importantly, there is less trial and error in your training sessions. An experienced trainer will be able to spot a problem and fix it before it develops into a bigger challenge. Poodles are such bright pupils that they will quickly learn how to avoid situations that they don't like, and a professional trainer will be able to help you maintain your position as pack leader and reach your dog's potential. Sherri Regalbuto of Just Dogs with Sheri says, "The best advice for a new poodle guardian is to hire a positive trainer who will help you to train your poodle instead of allowing your poodle to train you." Whether you choose private lessons or group lessons, the trainer will be able to answer any questions you may have and help you work through any challenging behavior.

Private lessons are a wonderful opportunity for you and your dog to have the trainer's undivided attention. If you are working through any problem behaviors, this may be the ideal way to seek help. However, private lessons can be costly, so if you are on a budget you might want to consider group lessons. Although you won't have the trainer's undivided attention, you will still be able to receive the guidance and instruction you need. It can also be a great opportunity to socialize your dog and practice good behavior in distracting environments.

Remember, professional trainers will never judge you for seeking help with your dog. Whether you are dealing with serious behavior issues or can't seem to get your dog to walk politely on a leash, there is no shame in asking for help. Trainers love what they do, and they are always willing to help you and your dog develop a closer relationship. Allowing bad behavior to escalate will only make it more difficult to correct and may cause unnecessary stress and resentment among your family members. The sooner you seek help, the sooner you and your dog can have the relationship that you've always dreamed about.

Owner Behavior

When you and your dog are struggling with a certain task or behavior, it can be easy to blame everything on the dog. However, bad behaviors are often a reflection of the owner's behavior. It can be difficult, but it's essential that you reflect on your own behavior and hold yourself accountable when training isn't going according to your plan. If you're becoming frustrated, take

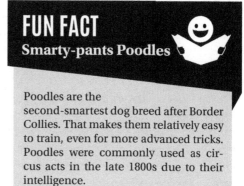

FUN FACT
Smarty-pants Poodles

Poodles are the second-smartest dog breed after Border Collies. That makes them relatively easy to train, even for more advanced tricks. Poodles were commonly used as circus acts in the late 1800s due to their intelligence.

a break and think about your own body language and whether or not there is something you could change that might make a difference in your dog's behavior. Training problems are often a result of miscommunication and there may be changes you can make to help your dog understand what you are asking of him.

If you've reflected on your own behavior and can't seem to find the problem, try having a trainer or dog savvy friend watch one of your training sessions. You may be missing something, and having an extra set of eyes on you can help you figure it out. Perhaps you don't realize how much tension you have in your body when you grip your dog's leash, or you may be walking too far from your dog. Having another person can help you sort out the details in your training that may otherwise go unnoticed. It's always helpful to seek a second opinion, especially that of a professional.

CHAPTER 11
Basic Commands

"Poodle are very easy to train. This can go either direction too. You can 'be trained' by your Poodle, or you can train your Poodle. Rule 1 is KNOW WHAT YOU WANT before you ask it. Then follow through with what you asked and BE CONSISTENT! Never be in a hurry when training you Poodle. Always take the time to do it correctly and follow through every time or your pup will see a way around your commands and do as they please. Be a good leader, and always be fair."

LeeAnna Springer
Springer Clan Standard Poodles

Benefits of Proper Training

One of the greatest benefits of properly training your Poodle is the mental stimulation your poodle derives from his training sessions. Poodles are intelligent dogs that need to use their minds regularly or they'll gladly find less desirable ways to entertain themselves. Training sessions do not need to be lengthy to provide mental stimulation and strengthen the bond you have with your dog. Sessions as short as five minutes can be held throughout the day. These short sessions are enough to work your dog's brain without overwhelming him. Regular training sessions will result in a calmer, happier dog who is eager to learn anything you want to teach him.

Proper training will also help your dog learn how to behave himself in new situations. When combined with proper socialization, proper training can help you create a dog that can go anywhere and handle anything. Whether you plan on traveling with your dog or competing at dog shows, you can be confident that your dog will be on his best behavior. Being able to go everywhere with you will also make your Poodle happier and will provide him with even more mental stimulation. Poodles love spending time with their owners, but it's your responsibility to make sure that your Poodle is well-behaved and can accompany you to work or on your errands without causing any disturbances.

Different Training Methods

If you were to ask ten different dog trainers about their training method of choice, you would likely get ten different answers. There are many different methods and each trainer will typically do things a little different from the next. It's up to you to do your research and try out different methods to see what works for you and your dog. What works for your neighbor and her Poodle may not work for you and yours. There is likely to be some trial and error in finding your ideal method, so don't be afraid to try out different methods. You may need to try out a variety of treats, toys, or reinforcements. As always,

Photo Courtesy of
Rachael Mavroudis

if you have any doubts about your abilities or simply need some professional advice, don't be afraid to seek the opinion of a qualified professional.

Basic Commands

The commands you can teach your Poodle are limited only by your imagination. Your Poodle will happily work with you to learn anything you want to teach him. As Mary Ann Riess of Vision Red Standard Poodles puts it, "Poodles are incredibly intelligent. They really do love to learn." Teaching your dog new commands is also a great form of mental stimulation and it will strengthen your relationship. To start with, there are a few basic commands that every dog needs to know. These commands will be easy for your Poodle to learn, but they will make life with your new dog much easier. Basic commands are not only the first step in training for any sport, but they also teach your dog good manners. Whether you are raising a future obedience show-ring star or simply a family pet, your Poodle will need to know simple commands such as sit, lie down, and walking on a loose leash.

Sit

Photo Courtesy of Vicki Farndell

The 'sit' command is one of the first commands that most dogs are taught, simply because it's one of the easiest. It can be used as the starting point for many other commands and tricks as well. It also puts your dog in a position where he can look up at you more easily, allowing him to see your next instructions. When combined with a 'stay' or 'wait' command, 'sit' can be used to teach your dog patience when eating dinner or exiting the house.

There are a few different methods of teaching your dog to sit. You can use each method separately or combine them in a way that works best for you and your dog. The first method is a type of positive reinforcement. You take a high-value treat and hold it just above your dog's head, but not so high that he feels that he must jump to reach it. Most dogs will quickly learn that they can put themselves at the right angle to reach the treat by sitting down. You can also use two different types of negative reinforcement. You can either put gentle pressure on your dog's hips with your hand as you give the treat or gently pull up on your dog's leash as you give the sit command. As soon as your Poodle sits, be sure to release the pressure immediately and reward him.

Stay

The 'stay' command is an especially useful command for any Poodle to know. It teaches your dog patience and self-control. The stay can be performed sitting, lying down, or standing. Some Poodle owners use two different commands, depending on how long they want their dog to wait and how they plan on releasing him from the command. 'Stay' can be used for long periods of time and you will typically release the dog by returning to the same po-

Photo Courtesy of Emil Friberg

sition in which you asked the dog to stay, for example, by his side or in front of him. 'Wait' can be used for short periods of time and the dog can be released from anywhere. You can use this command when working on recalls or when asking your dog to wait politely for his food dish. As the dog progresses in his training, you can ask him to stay for longer periods of time and you can gradually increase the distance between you and the dog. You can also introduce distractions and perform the command in new locations.

Stay can be taught more easily once your dog knows how to sit and lie down. Ask your dog to sit, stand, or lie down and give him the 'stay' or 'wait' command. Pause for a second or two and if he stays in place, you can reward him. If he moves out of position, simply put him back in place and try again. Corrections are not helpful in the beginning stages of 'stay,' so it's best to just start over. As your dog begins to understand what you are expecting of him, you can increase the time you ask him to stay. You can also begin taking a step or two away from him and even leave the room as his training advances. You can also use distractions, such as rolling his favorite ball across the room or tossing treats onto the floor out of his reach.

Lie Down

Lying down is a useful command for your dog to know, both at home and out on the town. You may need to ask your dog to lie down in the car, at the vet, or when he becomes a little too excited about meeting new friends. It's typically the second command, after sit, that puppies learn because it's easy to progress to the 'down' command once the puppy knows how to sit. It's a requirement in competition obedience and agility, and is also the precursor to many tricks, such as 'roll over' and 'crawl.'

As with the sit command, you can use positive or negative reinforcement, or a combination of the two. With positive reinforcement, you simply lure the dog into position with a treat. Ask your Poodle to sit and hold a treat in front of his nose to draw his attention. As he tries to reach for the treat, lower your hand to the ground. He should follow the treat with his nose into the correct position. If he doesn't lie down, or he stands and puts his head down instead, simply start from the beginning. To use negative reinforcement, ask your dog to sit while wearing his collar and leash. Put gentle downward pressure on the leash and release as soon as he begins to lie down. Once he's lying down, you can praise and reward him.

Come

Photo Courtesy of Marc Lang

The recall, or 'come' command, is one of the most important commands you can teach your Poodle. It is essential for any dog, whether he's a show dog or a beloved pet, to reliably come when he's called. If you ever plan on having your dog off-leash at a dog park or while hiking, he will need to have a solid recall to prevent any tragedies from happening. Most dog sports require dogs to be off-leash at the more advanced levels, so the recall will be a necessary part of your future competitors training. Even dogs who are not off-leash regularly can benefit from learning how to come when called, just in case of emergencies.

This command is best taught using two people, so if you have a friend or family member that can help you, you'll find that your dog will progress much more quickly. It's also best to work on your recall in an enclosed space, such as a large room or yard, to begin with. If you want to work on this command in an unfenced area, it may be worthwhile to invest in a tracking lead, which is simply an extra-long leash that will allow you to give your dog some freedom but won't allow him to run away. Have your assistant hold your dog while you stand some distance away. This is one command where it's okay for your dog to be a little excited, so don't be afraid to act a little silly to entice your dog. Ask him to come. Then pat your knees, or whistle if you have to. Your puppy should be excited by this and will struggle and try to reach you. Ask your helper to hold onto the dog for just a moment to help build the excitement. When your helper releases the dog, back up a few steps as he runs toward you. This forces your dog to chase you, if only for a few steps, and it can increase your dog's energy and level of excitement. Once your puppy reaches you, praise him and reward him. Don't be afraid to be a little over the top during these initial training sessions. Now that the dog is with you, you can hold onto him while your assistant asks him to come. You can do this back and forth for a few minutes, but your puppy may get tired quickly. As your Poodle advances in his recall training, you can increase the distance he has to cover to reach you. You can also practice in more distracting environments such as a park or field.

Off/Down

The 'off' or 'down' command is an essential part of your dog's training, as it will help you to establish and maintain your position as pack leader. The leader of the pack gets to choose where to sleep or sit, so use this command confidently when asking your Poodle to move out of your favorite chair or side of the bed. This is also a useful command when teaching your dog the rules of the house. Some Poodles may try to jump onto tables, countertops, or the laps of your guests. Remember to differentiate this command from the one you use to ask him to lie down. If you use 'down' for lying down, try to use a different word, such as 'off,' when asking him to get back onto the floor.

There are a few different methods you can use to encourage your dog to get off the furniture. First, you can try to lure him off with a treat while giving your chosen verbal command. Once all four paws are on the ground, you can reward him. You can also use a collar and leash or slip lead. Use gentle pressure on the leash to encourage your dog to move off the chair or sofa. Again, once he's on the ground, you can praise and reward him. You can also try using your hand to gently push him off, but use caution with dogs who have aggression or resource-guarding problems, as they may try to bite you. If your dog displays this type of behavior, you should also avoid grabbing his collar to pull him off.

Give/Drop

Photo Courtesy of Juan Barrionuevo

Poodles are retrievers, so they have a tendency to pick things up and carry them in their mouth. Unfortunately, they don't always choose appropriate items. The 'give' or 'drop' command is crucial to your dog's training. If you plan on competing with your dog, he may need to know this command in the show ring. It's also helpful to discourage your dog from picking up things off the sidewalk on walks or around the house. Mischievous Poodles sometimes try to steal things around the house and can be stubborn about giving them back. A solid 'give' or 'drop' command also discourages your dog from developing resource-guarding issues.

It's important that you avoid trying to take the item directly out of your dog's mouth. He may try to run from you, or he may try to snap at you. Instead, give him your chosen command and offer him a treat. Once he drops the item in favor of the treat, you can quickly grab whatever you've asked him to drop. If it's an item he's allowed to have, you can simply give it back to him. Eventually, the dog should learn that if he drops whatever is in his mouth, he will be rewarded.

Walk

Walking a dog who is constantly pulling on the leash can be stressful and exhausting, especially with a larger dog such as a Standard Poodle. Additionally, the dog may be able to hurt himself by pulling too hard on his collar or harness. Dogs who pull on the leash are also more likely to develop other behavior problems, such as excessive barking or aggression toward other dogs or strangers. No matter how cute or friendly your Poodle may be, strangers are unlikely to be charmed when they see him straining on the leash and lunging toward them, even if it's out of excitement rather than aggression.

It can be helpful, especially with energetic and excitable puppies, to hold a quick play session before practicing good leash manners. Otherwise, your dog may be too excited to focus on you and what you're asking of him. For this reason, it's also best to begin working on leash manners at home in a controlled environment. As your dog advances in his training, you can begin practicing around the neighborhood or at the local park or hiking trail. Begin walking with your Poodle on the leash and the moment he begins to pull, simply stop walking. He will likely turn around to look at you, wondering why you've stopped. Ask him to come back to you and reward him when he does so. Once there is slack in the leash again, try walking for a few steps. If he begins to pull, repeat the process. In the beginning, you may not be able to go more than a few steps at a time before your Poodle starts pulling, but eventually you will be able to go further without stopping. After a few sessions at home, you can try taking your Poodle out for longer walks around the neighborhood and introduce more distractions.

Advanced Commands

The sky is the limit when it comes to teaching your Poodle more advanced commands. They are such intelligent dogs; they will learn anything you want to teach them. You can increase the challenge of any of the basic commands by increasing the distractions or practicing in different environments. Try working on your down-stays at the local park or practice loose-leash walking at the local farmers market. If you plan on competing with your dog, try working on commands that are specific to your chosen sport. If you are not interested in competition, you can try teaching him a few tricks. The AKC even offers a trick dog class if you want to combine your love of competition with your desire to teach your dog interesting commands.

HELPFUL TIP
Beyond the Basics

Once your Poodle has learned the basic commands, use your imagination and your dog's intelligence to teach it a wide variety of tricks. Not only is that fun for you, but your Poodle will be grateful to have a way to use its intelligence in a way that pleases you.

CHAPTER 12
Unwanted Behaviors

"Poodles will rule your house if you do not condition them to be the second in command."

Martha Carroll-Talley
Custom Poodles

What is Bad Behavior in Dogs?

Photo Courtesy of Bec Bland

Any unwanted, destructive, or harmful behavior can be considered bad behavior. This can include chewing up furniture and personal items, excessive barking, and aggression. Bad behavior can be relatively harmless, yet still rude and disrespectful. Pulling on the leash, or jumping on guests, for instance, can be frustrating but there is not really any danger to you or your dog. However, bad behavior has a tendency to escalate and if left unchecked, you may find yourself with an unmanageable or aggressive dog. Behavior such as bolting out the door, growling, or snapping at strangers puts your Poodle and anyone near him in danger. Bad behavior must be corrected at the first sign to prevent it from escalating into a more dangerous and difficult to fix situation.

Typically, dogs develop bad habits because their owners let seemingly harmless behavior go unchecked. They may think it's cute when their tiny Toy Poodle growls at the neighbor, or when their adorable puppy starts carrying around a favorite pair of shoes, but before they know it, their dog is biting the neighborhood children and shredding valuable items. Extremely destructive or harmless behavior doesn't develop overnight. It takes time and a lack of correction for dogs to become unmanageable. Some owners may not feel comfortable correcting their dogs, but it's an important aspect of responsibly raising a respectful and well-behaved dog. Dogs must have boundaries, and those boundaries must be consistent. If you are not correcting your dog every time he behaves badly, he will only become confused about why he's allowed to act this way sometimes, but at other times he is corrected. Extremely bad habits take a significant amount of time and effort to correct, but they can easily be prevented if you are consistent about your training from the beginning.

Finding the Root of the Problem

You will never be able to completely correct your dog's bad behavior if you don't understand why he acts the way he does. If you know your dog barks aggressively only when he sees other dogs on walks, but he's fine with other dogs at home, you will know where you need to focus your training. However, if you have no idea why your dog has started snapping at strangers, you may not be able to completely correct the problem. You might be able to improve the situation, but without knowing the specific stimuli that is triggering your dog's behavior, you'll never be able to completely eliminate the problem.

Photo Courtesy of Sherri-Ann Harris

One of the most important and overlooked reason for a dog's bad habits is an owner's behavior. It can be easy to blame all of your dog's problems on him, but it's important to consider your own behavior and whether the way you are managing your dog might be the cause. Poodles adore their owners and tend to notice even the most subtle changes in human body language. If they sense that you are not confident and may not be able to handle a situation, they may believe that they need to step up and defend you or handle the situation themselves. However, if you approach new or scary situations with confidence, your dog is more likely to trust you to han-

Photo Courtesy of Regana Jones

dle it and take care of him. Though owner behavior is not the cause of every dog's problem behavior, it's an important aspect to consider when trying to find the root of your Poodle's bad habits.

Another often overlooked cause of problem behaviors is how the dog's environment is managed. If your dog likes to become destructive while you're gone, especially if he has access to the entire house, then you need to take control of the situation by limiting his access or keeping him in a crate while you're away from home. By controlling your dog's environment, you will be better able to predict his behavior and correct it if he acts up. Depending on the severity of your dog's problems, this may be a lifetime commitment, particularly if your dog exhibits signs of aggression. If you are committed to fixing your dog's bad behavior, you must take the necessary steps to manage his environment so that you can focus on his correcting his reactions.

Bad Behavior Prevention

It's often easier to prevent a problem behavior from developing than it is to correct it, but you must be consistent. Properly managing your dog's environment and behavior from the beginning can seem like a time-consuming hassle, but in the long run, you'll be happy you put the time and effort into your dog's training. Proper management consists of understanding where your dog is in his training and adjusting his surroundings accordingly. If you know that your Poodle likes to chew up your shoes, either pick up your shoes or keep him contained in a smaller section of the house or in his crate.

Preventing bad behaviors and managing your dog's surroundings will also make it easier for you to establish and maintain your position as pack leader. Each time that you let your dog get away with a bad behavior, he will become more confident that he is the leader of your household. Martha Carroll-Talley of Custom Poodles says, "They will rule your house if you don't condition them to be second-in-command." Make sure you practice strong leadership from the moment you bring your Poodle home. If you make sure that you are always the first to walk through a doorway, your Poodle is less likely to develop a habit of bolting out open doors. If you teach him to wait patiently for his dinner, he will also be less likely to become a resource guarder. On the other hand, if you allow him to rush through doorways or bully you for food, you're going to end up with a dog who is difficult to manage and you will need to work even harder to erase the bad habits that you have allowed to develop.

How to Properly Correct Your Poodle

When you correct your Poodle's bad behavior, it's essential that you maintain a gentle touch and positive attitude. Bad behavior can be frustrating, but if you lose your temper, you may do more harm than good. There is no situation in which it is appropriate to hit or kick your Poodle. Your aggressive behavior is likely to be met with an aggressive reaction from your dog and you may be bitten. Your dog may become fearful of you, or even humans in general. Even the most severe behavioral problems can be improved with patience and a gentle touch, so if you find it difficult to maintain your composure during corrections, you may want to contact a professional trainer who can help you find a way to correct your dog's behavior without anyone getting upset.

When correcting your Poodle's mistakes, it's important to remember that you can only correct the dog if you catch him in the act. If you come home and find that your throw pillows have been torn to pieces, this is not an appropriate time to punish your dog. You will simply have to clean up the mess and hope you catch him next time. Dogs do not have the same understanding of past events that humans do. Your Poodle will not understand that you are angry with him for tearing up the pillows and he will not associate any punishment with his previous actions. However, if you come home and see your Poodle with a throw pillow in his mouth, then it is an appropriate time for a correction.

Even if you catch your dog in the act, it's crucial that your correction is only as harsh as necessary. Overcorrecting your dog may only result in fear, rather than behavior modification. Loud claps or stomps, or a firm 'no' are usually sufficient to interrupt your dog's behavior. Many trainers also recommend filling a small spray bottle with water and spritzing your dog in the face when he acts inappropriately. Dogs don't usually appreciate a sudden spurt of water in their face, so it's a sufficient but harmless correction. Although the water won't hurt your dog, it is a stronger form of correction than just saying 'no,' so use your best judgment to determine which behaviors warrant this type of correction. For more serious problems, such as fighting, you may need harsher corrections. Spraying the dogs with a hose, yelling, or banging metal food bowls together are appropriate in these situations. Poodles, especially the smaller varieties, can be seriously injured or even killed in a dog fight, so it's important to adjust your level of correction accordingly.

Fixing Bad Habits

Patience is a crucial part of fixing your Poodle's bad habits. His naughty behavior didn't develop overnight, and it won't be fixed overnight either. It may take weeks or even months of consistent management and correction before you see any significant improvements. Whether you are attempting to solve the problem yourself or are working with a professional, it's important to understand that it will take time for your dog to develop new habits, just as it took time for him to develop his bad habits. It can be frustrating to stay committed to your training plan, especially when you don't see improvements quickly, but you must be patient and try not to lose your motivation.

Consistency is another essential aspect of correcting problem behaviors. It can be difficult to stay committed to your dog's training plan, especially when your work or family life become stressful, but if you want to solve your dog's problems, you must stay focused and committed. A lack of consistency is how your dog developed his bad habits, so you must now be more consistent than ever to help him form more desirable habits. Depending on the severity of your dog's behavior, you may need to practice this level of behavior management for his entire life, so be prepared to dedicate a lot of your time to your dog's training, especially if you are dealing with serious aggression or fear issues.

When to Call a Professional

Some owners may think that the only time it's appropriate to call a professional is when their dog's behavior gets out of hand, but in reality, professional trainers can help you at any point in your dog's training. If you aren't sure about the appropriate level of correction, or your timing, call a trainer and discuss your problems. They can help you develop a training plan that is best suited for your dog and his specific bad habits. Catching bad behavior in its early stages often means it's easier and less time-consuming to correct, so don't be afraid to contact a professional at the first sign.

If your dog is displaying any type of dangerous behavior, you need to call a professional trainer or behaviorist immediately. Aggressive, destructive, or fearful behavior can escalate quickly, potentially leading to tragedy, so it's essential that you seek professional help as soon as possible. Most Poodle owners are not equipped to deal with serious behavioral problems, so the sooner your dog receives professional help, the better. If your dog is displaying aggressive behavior toward humans, he could become a liability as he may bite you, your family, or a complete stranger. Aggression toward other dogs may result in your dog becoming seriously injured or even killed, especially if he's a Toy or Miniature Poodle. Professional trainers and behaviorists work with aggressive and fearful dogs on a regular basis and they will have the knowledge and tools necessary to help your dog overcome his problems.

Poodle-specific Bad Habits

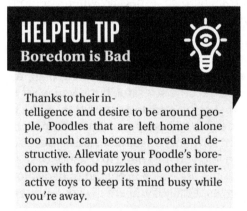

HELPFUL TIP
Boredom is Bad

Thanks to their intelligence and desire to be around people, Poodles that are left home alone too much can become bored and destructive. Alleviate your Poodle's boredom with food puzzles and other interactive toys to keep its mind busy while you're away.

Many bad habits that are specific to the breed are related to their history as retrievers. Most puppies explore the world with their mouth, but Poodles can be especially mouthy, especially as puppies. You may find that your Poodle chews on inappropriate items or bites too hard during play. Poodles will often take things in their mouth and run off with them, playing hard to get. It's important to discourage this type of behavior in its early stages. Most Poodle puppies don't bite out of aggression, it's simply how they play, and sometimes they may play too rough. Likewise, chewing and stealing are not done out of malice, but rather as a way to entertain themselves. Still, these habits are annoying and disrespectful, so be sure to encourage your dog to express his playful side in other ways.

Poodles adore their owners and make excellent family dogs. Unfortunately, their dedication to their families often evolves into separation anxiety. Excessive barking is a common problem with Poodles, especially when they are left alone. This can be a particularly difficult habit to break, so prevention is key. From the first day that you bring your Poodle home, you must remember not to make a big deal about leaving or coming home. The less concerned you are about leaving your Poodle, the less concerned he will be. Poodles are a social breed, so it may also be helpful to have another dog or other animal at home to keep them company, so consider adopting another pet if you're concerned about leaving your Poodle home alone for long periods of time.

Size-specific Bad Habits

Toy and Miniature Poodles are prone to developing 'small dog syndrome.' This is a collection of behaviors that is frequently more tolerated in small dogs than in big dogs. Excessive barking, growling at strangers, and resource guarding are found more frequently in small dogs, simply because the dogs don't present as much of a threat as larger dogs, so the behaviors are not corrected with the same consistency. To prevent your Toy or Miniature Poodle from developing small dog syndrome, it's important that you practice firm and consistent leadership. Make sure your Poodle knows you are the leader of the pack. If you make it clear that you are in charge, your Poodle is less likely to feel the need to take over that position.

Standard Poodles often have a reputation of being high-strung or neurotic, but it is more often due to a lack of physical and mental exercise. Due to the Poodle's prissy appearance, many people incorrectly assume that the dogs do not need much stimulation. However, Poodles are highly intelligent and athletic dogs that crave stimulation. The more physical and mental exercise your Standard Poodle receives, the more well-behaved he will be. Proper socialization and training will also help your Poodle learn how to appropriately interact with other dogs and people.

CHAPTER 13
Traveling with Poodles

"A poodle of any size loves to travel. They are bred to be a companion dog and love to be around their owners and going on new adventures."

Martha Carroll-Talley
Custom Poodles

Dog Carriers and Car Restraints

HELPFUL TIP
Traveling Tips

The ease of traveling with your Poodle will depend on the size of the Poodle you have. A Toy Poodle will fit under an airline seat and should be welcome at any hotel that allows dogs. A Standard Poodle, on the other hand, will need to fly in cargo and won't be welcome at some dog-friendly hotels that have size restrictions on the dogs they allow. Plan your travel accordingly.

Traveling with your Poodle can be a wonderful experience for both of you, but it's important to take some time to consider your safety options. An unrestrained dog in the car is not only a danger to himself but also to everyone else in the car and on the road. If your dog does not have a solid recall, there's also a chance he could escape during an accident or simply when you open the car door. A dog who is an inexperienced travel can become panicked or carsick, distracting you from the road. Using a safety device will allow you to focus on driving without having to worry about your dog. There are many different options available, so you may want to try a few different methods to see which one works best for you and your dog.

For the smaller varieties of Poodle, a booster seat is an excellent option for traveling in a car. Booster seats are typically made of firm foam or plastic and can be attached to your car's seat with the seat belt. These seats will elevate your dog enough that he can see out the car window but he will be safely restrained, with his harness clipped to the seat. Some dogs feel more comfortable when they are able to see what is happening around them, so it may help your dog settle down in the car. If you dog is easily overwhelmed, he may prefer a different method of restraint. These seats are usually quite small and typically don't work well with Standard Poodles.

Kennels are one of the most popular choices for Poodles of all sizes. You have the option of metal, plastic, or mesh fabric crates. Some crates are made specifically for use in cars, but some owners just use their dog's regular plastic or wire crate. Travel can be an exciting and potentially overwhelming experience, especially for puppies, but dogs who have been properly crate trained may find comfort and a sense of security in their kennel. Crates also keep the dog safely contained should

Photo Courtesy of Kamesha Riggs

you have an accident. If your dog is prone to carsickness, crates are also an excellent way to contain the mess, making it easier to clean up after you arrive at your destination.

If your dog is most comfortable riding in the car without the confines of a kennel, a seat belt might be your best option. Doggy seat belts are typically just a short leash that attaches to your car's seat the same way a regular seat belt would. The other end of the leash attaches to your dog's harness. The leashes are usually long enough to give the dog enough space to stand up and turn around, but not enough that he can jump into the front seat or out an open window. When using a seat belt, remember to always attach the leash to your dog's harness, not his collar. Should you get into an accident or even just slam on the brakes, your dog could be badly injured or killed by the sudden pressure from the collar. A harness will distribute that pressure evenly, reducing the chances that your dog could become injured.

Preparing Your Poodle for Car Rides

FUN FACT
Sled-Dog Poodles

In 1988, musher John Suter entered the famous Iditarod sled dog race in Alaska with a team entirely composed of Standard Poodles. Thanks to frozen paws and matted fur, the team didn't do very well, leading to a new rule that only northern breeds of dogs like Alaskan Malamutes and Siberian Huskies are allowed to run the race.

Before you take your Poodle for his first road trip, you need to consider his prior experience with traveling and evaluate how you should prepare him. If he has ridden in the car in the past, you should have some idea of how comfortable he is with it. If he hasn't traveled with you much, you may need to spend some extra time getting him ready for a long car trip. Dogs who are inexperienced travelers often become carsick, especially if the road has a lot of winding turns or elevation changes. If you think your dog could become carsick, you need to prepare accordingly. Bringing a few towels or extra blankets, along with a plastic bag will help with cleanup if necessary. Lining your dog's kennel with washable blankets or even disposable puppy pads will also help. If your dog is traveling in a seat belt, consider investing in a waterproof seat cover. They are a great option for keeping your car clean.

Before traveling, consider limiting your dog's food and water intake, especially if he is prone to carsickness. Taking away your dog's food and water an hour or two before departure will also allow you to drive further before stopping for a break. Depending on how far you are driving and how old your Poodle is, you will likely need to stop for a bathroom break every few hours. Young puppies should be kept to the same house-training schedule that you use at home. You shouldn't withhold water from your dog for the entire drive, but giving water in the car can be messy, so try giving your dog small drinks of water every time you stop for a bathroom break. This will be enough to keep him hydrated but will help limit any accidents or carsickness due to a full stomach.

Depending on how long you are staying away from home, you'll want to make sure you bring your dog's usual supplies. Travel can be stressful for a dog, especially one with limited travel experience, so it's important to keep using the same products you use at home. Bring your dog's normal bed or blankets if possible, and any toys that might give him comfort. Be sure to feed him the same food he normally eats to avoid any upset stomach. Try to stick to the same feeding schedule you have at home, if possible. The more familiarities you can include on your trip, the more comfortable your Poodle will be on his first road trip.

Flying and Hotel Stays

Flying with a dog can be a complicated, stressful, and expensive experience, but the joy of having your Poodle with you on vacation can make it worth your while. Whether you're flying domestic or international, check to make sure your dog is up-to-date on all of his core vaccines. Make sure your destination does not have any specific requirements such as deworming or a rabies titer. Ask your vet about whether you'll need a health certificate. This is generally just a statement from your veterinarian that explains that your dog is healthy enough for air travel. You'll want to get a paper copy of all of your dog's health records to keep with you as well as a copy to keep with your dog and his crate. You should also notify your airline that you'll be traveling with a dog. Most airlines charge a small fee, so you'll need to ask whether you pay this before your flight or when you get to the airport. Preflight preparation can be one of the most stressful aspects of air travel with a dog, so make sure you've completed all of the necessary paperwork before flying.

If you have a small Poodle, such as a Toy or a smaller Miniature, you may be able to fly with him in the cabin. However, larger dogs must fly in the plane's cargo hold, so Standard Poodles, and possibly larger Miniature Poodles will likely fly this way. If your dog is traveling in cabin, he will need to travel in an airline-approved carrier. Check with your specific airline in ad-

Photo Courtesy of
Jasper Roam

Photo Courtesy of Karen Gallo

vance to make sure your carrier is the right size and type. Most airlines recommend soft-sided carriers for in-cabin travel. If your larger Poodle is traveling in the cargo hold, he will also need to fly in an airline-approved carrier, but it will need to be a sturdy plastic or metal crate. Before you fly, make sure your dog is comfortable spending time in his travel crate or carrier. Have him spend time in the crate at home, or even take him for a short car trip in it. As with regular crate training, you want to be patient with this process. You'll need to start getting your dog used to his carrier several weeks before your trip.

If you plan on staying in a hotel with your Poodle once you've reached your destination, make sure you're staying in pet-friendly accommodations. Some hotels do not allow dogs, while others will set up a bed, food and water bowls, and even treats, so do some research to make sure you're staying somewhere that will welcome your Poodle. Depending on the individual hotel, there may be a small fee for allowing your dog to stay. This fee is typically less than $50 per night, but if you're traveling on a budget this can be an unfortunate surprise. Some hotels also have weight restrictions on the pets that stay there, so if you're traveling with a Standard Poodle, you should ask about this when you make your reservation. Most importantly, make sure you've done your homework with training and socializing your dog. Even pet-friendly hotels will be displeased if you bring in a dog that is barking excessively or lunging at other guests. You want to make sure that you and your dog are respectful guests that will be welcomed back at any hotel.

Kenneling vs. Dog Sitters

Even if you usually travel with your Poodle, there may be an occasion where you need to leave him at home. In this case, it's important to find a boarding kennel or dog sitter who can be trusted to care for your precious pet in your absence. Depending on your area, you may find a range of boarding kennels and pet sitters. Some facilities are relatively simple, while others may offer all the comforts of home. The prices of such facilities will likely reflect the level of service they offer. Some boarding kennels keep the dogs comfortable in their kennels with bathroom breaks every few hours, while others may be entirely cage-free and staffed 24/7. In the latter case, the dogs are typically kept as a group and allowed to interact around the clock. If you think your dog would prefer a homier environment, consider hiring a pet sitter. Sitters will typically either stay at your home while you're gone or keep your dog in their own home. Consider your Poodle's personality and preferences when deciding which option to go with.

Depending on the area in which you live and your budget, you may have a few different options for boarding kennels. The cheaper options will usually keep your dog in a cage or kennel, usually with a separate run. If you have multiple dogs, they may be able to stay together if the facility allows and your dogs get along. Higher-end facilities will have more options available to you. They may offer luxuries such as elevated beds, television, and individual or group playtime. They may also be staffed around the clock, allowing the dogs to spend their time together as a group rather than in cages. Before committing to a boarding kennel, consider your dog's personality and what options he would be happiest with. Outgoing, gregarious Poodles will be so happy to play in a group that they may forget that you've left them behind on your travels. More timid Poodles may find the experience stressful and they may need quieter arrangements to keep them happy in your absence. Many boarding kennels also offer a trial day to make sure that your dog will be happy, so if you aren't sure how your dog will do, it's a good opportunity to find out.

Dog sitters are a great option for timid dogs or those who are easily stressed by change. This option allows them to stay in the comfort of their own homes, or the comfort of someone else's home, rather than in a kennel or cage. Pet-sitting companies can be found across the country and will provide you with a qualified and trustworthy pet sitter to stay in your home until you return. Self-employed sitters can also be found, who may take your dog into their own home. Pet sitters are also a great idea if you have other pets that need to be taken care of or plants that need to be watered. Many sitters are also happy to do small household chores like bringing in

Photo Courtesy of
Marc Lang

the mail or watering your garden. Their presence can also discourage potential thieves. Qualified pet sitters can be more expensive than traditional boarding kennels, but their exact price will vary based on location and the services they offer. Some pet sitters offer discounted rates for longer stays, as well.

If you choose to drop your dog off at either a boarding kennel or a pet sitter's home, remember to provide enough food for the entire time that you'll be gone, plus a little extra in case your return is delayed. It's also a good idea to check with the kennel staff or sitter to see what items you are allowed or encouraged to bring. Some places encourage boarders to bring blankets or toys from home, while others don't want to be responsible for any damage, so they provide their own. Whatever you bring with your dog, remember to label each and every item and keep a list of what you've left with your Poodle. This will help ensure that you come home with everything that you dropped off with your dog.

Tips and Tricks for Traveling

Traveling with your Poodle can be an exciting and rewarding experience if done properly. Terri L. Creech of Bear Cove Standard Poodles says, "Poodles are excellent traveling buddies. They love being with their people and seeing new things." Spending vacation time together with your Poodle and experiencing new things will help strengthen your bond and broaden your dog's horizons. However, you need to prepare yourself and your dog for your adventures. Making sure that your dog has a basic understanding of obedience commands and is relatively well socialized will help your trip go more smoothly. An under-socialized and untrained dog will be a nightmare to travel with and you will likely leave a bad impression on any hotel or airport staff.

Remember to bring all of your dog's necessary items, including medical information. It can help to write down a list in the weeks before your trip, so you don't forget anything at the last minute. You should bring enough food for the duration of your trip, as well as a little extra in case anything should delay your return. If your dog is more comfortable traveling with his own bed, blanket, or toys, be sure to include those on your list. Your dog's leash, collar, kennel, or seat belt will also be necessities. Don't forget to bring copies of your Poodle's vaccination information as well. You may not need this information, but if you do, you'll be happy you brought it along. It may also be helpful to keep your vet's contact information on hand. Some Poodle owners also choose to research vets in the city that they're traveling to, in case anything should happen. So much preparation before your trip can seem overwhelming, but embarking on a trip you haven't prepared for will be much more stressful. Make sure you've done everything you can to prepare your Poodle and your family for your trip together and you're sure to have the best trip possible.

CHAPTER 14
Nutrition

Importance of Good Diet

Feeding your Poodle a properly balanced diet will ensure that you are giving him the best chance at a long and healthy life. Without a balanced diet, your Poodle is at risk for developing potentially life-threatening conditions, especially as a puppy. Your dog must receive the proper amounts and ratios of essential vitamins and minerals in order to grow and develop strong bones and muscles. A proper diet also provides him with the nutrients to maintain a healthy immune system and a shiny coat. The various fats and proteins in a balanced diet also provide your dog with the necessary energy to perform in the show ring and play with his buddies. Not all dogs thrive on the same type of food, so you'll need to figure out what type of diet works best for your dog. Most commercial dog foods are formulated to standards set by the Association of American Feed Control Officials. AAFCO standards are designed to provide your dog with the nutrients required to live a long and healthy life.

A proper diet is essential to your Poodle's well-being, but a diet must also be balanced with portion control and adequate physical exercise. A well-balanced diet will not keep your dog healthy if he overeats and lounges on the sofa all day. Most commercial diets provide a rough guide on how much you should feed your dog based on his ideal weight. These guides are not always accurate since your dog's individual metabolism may differ from a similarly sized dog, but they offer a good starting point. In addition to portion control, be sure that your dog receives a minimum of 30 to 60 minutes of exercise per day. Exercise will not only help keep the excess weight off, but it will also keep your dog calm and relaxed.

HELPFUL TIP
Obesity

More than half of all dogs in the United States are overweight or obese, and obesity can cause many of the same problems in dogs that it causes in people. Obesity can even shorten your Poodle's life by a year or two. Make sure you're feeding your dog an appropriate amount of quality kibble—you should be able to feel your Poodle's ribs without too much effort.

Commercial dog food can be found in a number of different formulas. Some formulas are intended for dogs of all life stages, while others are formulated specifically for puppies or senior dogs. Puppy food tends to be higher in calories and has a different ratio of certain nutrients, while senior food is often lower in calories and sometimes contains nutrients intended to ease arthritis or other age-related conditions. There are also different formulas for different health concerns, such as kidney disease or allergies. As your dog ages, he may need to change foods occasionally due to changes in his health or overall well-being, so don't expect to keep your dog on the same type of food for his entire life. If you do need to change foods, most experts recommend a slow transition. Mary Ann Riess of Vision Red Standard Poodles says, "I do recommend that people go slow and introducing new foods to a puppy. It should be done over a long period of time, especially if you decide to change foods." Gradually introducing a new type of food will help ease any gastrointestinal distress and will also help picky eaters get used to their new food. The process of changing diets should be done over several days or a week, gradually increasing the percentage of new food and decreasing the percentage of old food.

Nutrition Differences in Size Varieties

There is little to no difference in the nutritional needs of the different-sized varieties of Poodle. The type of food you choose to feed your dog should be based on his individual needs and health concerns, rather than just his size. If you have multiple dogs in your home, you may find that your dogs may be able to all eat the same food, or they may each need a different diet. The biggest difference in dietary needs between the size varieties is their ability to eat large pieces of kibble. Toy Poodles may need a different-sized kibble than Standard Poodles. There are many different companies that make 'small bite' kibble specifically for Toy Breeds. Some Miniature Poodles handle regular-sized kibble well, while other prefer small bites, so you may need to try out different types of food to figure out what your dog likes best.

Another difference between the size varieties that you may encounter is that the amount of food your dog consumes is not directly related to his size. A Standard Poodle weighing 50 pounds will not eat exactly five times that of a Toy Poodle weighing ten pounds, nor will two 30-pound dogs eat the same amount. Small dogs often have higher metabolisms than larger dogs, but your dog's individual caloric needs will be different from other dogs of a similar size. Instead, you should base your dog's meal size on how active he is. If your Poodle runs with you every morning and also competes in agility and flyball on the weekends, he will obviously need more food than your neighbor's Poodle who takes a leisurely walk around the neighborhood twice a day. Some dogs may also be more active during certain times of the year, so you may need to adjust your dog's portions throughout the year. Keep an eye on your dog's weight and adjust his meal sizes accordingly.

Many adult Poodles of all size varieties fare well with one meal per day, while others prefer two, but small Toy Poodles may particularly need to eat more frequently, especially as puppies. Small dogs often have a difficult time regulating their blood sugar as efficiently as bigger dogs and frequent meals can help prevent serious drops in blood sugar levels. Puppies should always be fed more frequently than adults, but your dog's individual needs and preferences will dictate the ideal number of meals needed per day.

Different Types of Commercial Food

"Feed your Poodle in the morning and at night a specific amount so that you can keep track of what they are eating. I personally use Costco's Natures Domain. It is nutritious and reasonably priced."

Bob and Penny Daugherty
Sundance Poodles

The type of food you are probably most familiar with is kibble. The small, crunchy nuggets make up the majority of the pet food market and are available in a huge variety of sizes, flavors, and formulas. Most companies offer different foods for different life stages, but some even go so far as to offer different foods for different breeds of dog. Grain-free kibble has become popular in recent years, replacing corn, wheat, and soy with alternative carbohydrates such as potatoes and peas. For dogs with food sensitivities you can also find kibble made from novel proteins such as kangaroo, salmon, and venison. There are different- sized kibble pieces for different-sized dogs and even different formulas made for dogs with health concerns. If your dog is suffering from allergies or heart problems, there's a kibble specifically designed to help. If your Poodle is particularly picky, you may need to try a few different types of kibble before you find something he enjoys. Just remember to transition your dog to the new food over a period of several days or a week.

Canned food is another popular choice for Poodle owners. It comes in nearly as many varieties as kibble but is softer and has a higher moisture content. Canned food is ideal for older dogs or those with few or no teeth. Some dogs find canned food to be more palatable so it may be a helpful addition to a picky eater's meal. Canned food is also a great way to help hydrate dogs who don't drink enough water. However, because of its soft texture, canned food often sticks to dogs' teeth, leading to more plaque and tartar than with kibble. The crunchy texture of kibble often helps to scrape this off, so if your dog is strictly eating canned food, he may need more frequent teeth brushing or dental cleanings.

You may notice that your local pet store now has a refrigerated section. This is due to the rise in popularity of fresh dog food. Fresh dog food is typically packaged in a dense roll, which can be sliced according to your dog's portion needs. This is a great option for picky eaters or for owners who like the idea of a homecooked meal but lack the time or adequate understanding of nutrition. Fresh food is usually firmer than canned food, but softer than kibble, so it's also an option for dogs with missing teeth or older dogs. Be aware that fresh food is often more expensive than most canned food or kibble.

Another trend in dog food that can be found in your local pet store's refrigerated section is the raw diet. Raw food is intended to mimic the diet that dogs eat in the wild. Since kibble has not been around for very long, the raw diet is meant to return your dog to the diet of his ancestors. Commercial raw diets are usually small nuggets or patties made from a mixture of meat, organs, bone, and vegetables. Raw diets do not include grains or excess carbohydrates. Many raw feeders supplement their dog's diet with goat milk or recreational bones. Since raw food is quite soft, plaque and tartar can build up quickly, so the raw bones are meant to help clean the teeth. Like other diets, raw diets are available in a variety of proteins to suit dogs with different preferences and sensitivities.

Photo Courtesy of Alice Goodman

Homemade Foods and Recipes

Homemade diets are trending among Poodle owners who are dissatisfied with commercial options. Some owners choose to feed a homemade raw diet, while others prefer to cook their dog's food at home. Depending on your dog's needs, homemade diets can be expensive and labor intensive, so if you don't have a lot of spare time, you may need to consider a commercial diet. It's important to thoroughly research homemade diets before you start making your dog's food. Homemade diets can cause nutritional imbalances if not properly formulated. The effects on your dog's health will likely not show up right away, but they may cause long-term damage to your dog's well-being. If you aren't confident in the nutritional balance of your homemade diet or simply would like some professional guidance, consider consulting a canine nutritionist or a veterinarian that specializes in nutrition. They will be able to analyze the nutrients in your dog's food or even provide you with a nutritionally balanced recipe.

Cooked homemade diets can be a great option for picky Poodles or those with severe allergies or intolerances. You'll be able to decide on each and every ingredient that you include, so you won't have any surprise allergic reactions from your dog. Home-cooked diets typically include different types of meat, organs, and vegetables. They may also include some type of carbohydrate such as rice, oats, or even barley. Some owners also supplement their dogs' diets with various vitamins and minerals to ensure they're their dogs are getting all of the essential nutrients. If you are interested in learning more about home-cooked diets, there is an incredible variety of books that have been published about the subject. Many of these books also include recipes. You can also speak to a professional nutritionist or veterinarian for recommendations.

Raw diets are probably the most popular type of homemade diet among dog owners. Generally, raw diets are categorized as either Prey Model Raw (PMR) or Biologically Appropriate Raw Food (BARF). The reason for this is the debate on whether or not you should include vegetables in your dog's diet. PMR diets consist of meat, bones, and organs with little to no vegetables. The PMR diet and the percentages of meat, bone, and organ are intended to reflect the amounts that can be found in whole prey animals. BARF diets are similar, but they allow for up to 10 percent of the diet to consist of fruit and vegetables. Owners who make their own food may also supplement the diet with goat milk, bone broth, or fish stock for additional nutrients. On raw diets, dogs do consume a certain percentage of bone, which particularly small or senior dogs may struggle with, so some owners opt to grind their dogs' food, similar to commercial raw diets.

People Food – Harmful and Acceptable Kinds

Photo Courtesy of
Charlotte Haugen Ladegård

Some experts recommend keeping people food far away from your dog, while others only recommend certain foods and only in moderation. If people food makes up more than 10 percent of your dog's daily portion of food, you may find that his diet will become unbalanced over time. People food is best used for special occasions and as treats or rewards.

The healthiest types of people food to give your Poodle are fruits and vegetables. Most fruits and vegetables are low calorie and provide benefits such as essential vitamins and antioxidants. Fruit can be higher in sugar, so if your dog is sensitive to sugar, it may be best to limit his fruit consumption or stick with vegetables only. Fruits that are nontoxic for dogs include bananas, apples, blueberries, and cantaloupe. Many dogs also enjoy eating watermelon, pineapple, and raspberries. Healthy vegetables include sweet potatoes, carrots, celery, and cucumbers. Green beans and peas also make excellent treats. Broccoli and spinach can also be fed in moderation but may cause stomach upset in some dogs. Be cautious when introducing new fruits or vegetables to your dog's diet as some are toxic to dogs. Grapes, garlic, and onion can be harmful, especially if eaten in large amounts. The pits of pitted fruits such as peaches, mangoes, and cherries can also be harmful, but if the pit is removed the fruit can safely be fed to your Poodle.

There are also certain types of people food that can be fed, but only in small quantities. Cheese and peanut butter are popular treats for dogs but can be quite high in fat. The high fat content can affect some dog's endocrine systems, so these types of treats are best used only for special occasions. Salty foods such as ham, bacon, or popcorn should also be kept to a minimum. Some dogs are also quite sensitive to dairy products, especially in large amounts. Foods such as yogurt, kefir, or milk should be fed sparingly.

Most dog owners are aware of toxic foods such as chocolate and anything containing caffeine, but there are a few unexpected foods to watch out for. Food that contains the artificial sweetener xylitol should be avoided at all costs. Xylitol is commonly found in sugar-free candy and gum and is extremely toxic to dogs, even in relatively small amounts. It may seem obvious, but alcohol should also be avoided. If you think your dog may have eaten something toxic, it's important to contact your local veterinarian as soon as possible. The sooner he can be treated, the more likely he is to survive the ordeal.

Weight Management

One of the most common conditions affecting pets is obesity. Overweight dogs are prone to myriad other health problems including diabetes and heart disease. Obesity can also have a negative impact on your dog's ability to exercise and enjoy life. Excess weight also puts more stress on your dog's joints, which can lead to arthritis and mobility problems even at a young age. It can be tempting to spoil your Poodle, especially when he gives you that look that just melts your heart, but for your dog's health and well-being, you must choose to show your affection through petting and praise, rather than treats and snacks.

The recommended guidelines of what each size variety should weigh are meant to guide breeders toward developing consistency in the breed. They should not be used to determine whether your dog is the correct weight. Each dog is an individual and even littermates can vary in size. Depending on your Poodle's hairstyle, it may be difficult to determine whether he's at the correct weight. Long hair can be deceiving, so it's important to put your hands on the dog and feel his body. A healthy dog should have a slight but defined waist when viewed from above, or when felt along his sides. You should be able to feel his ribs, but they don't need to be visible, even with a short haircut. When viewed from the side, your dog should have a pronounced tuck up under the belly at the waist. Poodles are a deep-chested breed, so it's okay if this is more pronounced than in other breeds. If you are unsure about whether your dog is at his ideal weight, ask your veterinarian.

When calculating portions and determining your dog's daily food intake, it's crucial that you include all treats. Treats shouldn't make up more than 10 percent of your dog's diet, but they should always be included in his daily calorie allotment. If your dog needs to watch his waistline, but you spend a lot of time in training, you may be able to use a portion of his meals as his training reward. You can also substitute his treats for small bits of his favorite fruit or vegetable. It's also important to make sure your dog gets enough exercise every day. The more he exercises, the more he will be allowed to eat, so if you're set on spoiling your Poodle with treats, make sure he is exercising enough to keep his weight at a healthy and manageable number.

CHAPTER 15
Grooming Your Poodle

"Poodles need to be introduced to grooming when they are puppies usually 4-5 weeks of age. This way they get used to clippers, especially around the face. Brushing and combing their coat routinely will avoid matting and get them accustomed to being groomed. Once their puppy coat is gone and their adult coat comes in, they should be groomed every 6-8 weeks."

Sharon Hoffman
Hofman's Toys

Coat Basics

Poodles are known for their curly hair and extravagant styles, but the truth is that the Poodle's famous coat requires a lot of regular maintenance and grooming. Even if you don't keep your Poodle in the high-maintenance continental clip that you see in the show ring, he will still need frequent grooming to keep his coat healthy and mat-free. Sherri Hoffman of Hoffman's Toys recommends, "Once the puppy coat is gone and the adult coat is in, Poodles should be groomed every six to eight weeks." Many potential Poodle owners have changed their minds on the breed once they realize how much time and effort must be spent brushing their dogs. There's always the option of sending your dog to a professional groomer, but this may not be an option for a Poodle owner on a tight budget.

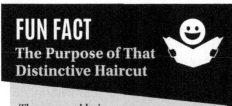

FUN FACT
The Purpose of That Distinctive Haircut

The unusual haircut you see on Poodles in the show ring actually has a historical purpose. Hunters who used Poodles to retrieve birds for them wanted their dogs to have less fur to drag them down while they were in the water, but they also wanted enough hair left to keep the dogs' organs and joints warm in cold water. That's why the chest is left long, and the pompons on the hips and ankles protect the joints.

All sizes of adult Poodles have dense, coarse coats that grow in tight curls. The tightness of the coat's curls, or ringlets, can vary from Poodle to Poodle. They are a single-coated breed, which simply means that their coat grows in a single layer, rather than the undercoat and guard hairs of other breeds like Huskies and German Shepherds. Poodles are often referred to as hypoallergenic dogs because they don't shed, but this isn't entirely true. Poodles do shed, but the shed hair is often caught in the curls of coat, so it doesn't end up all over your house as with other breeds. This shed hair can lead to tangles and mats quickly if it isn't brushed out on a regular basis.

Poodle puppies' coats differ from their adult counterparts in both texture and curliness. Puppies often have a wavy coat, rather than the tight curls of adult dogs. Their hair is often much softer than an adult's as well. Between nine and 18 months of age, puppies begin to shed their puppy coat as their curlier, coarser adult coat comes in. It is essential that you brush and groom your puppy regularly during this period as mats can develop quickly.

Bathing and Brushing

Brushing your Poodle's coat on a regular basis is one of the most important and time-consuming aspects of Poodle care. Even if you keep your Poodle in a relatively short hairstyle, you must still brush him frequently and thoroughly to prevent mats from developing. It's also important to make sure that your Poodle is mat-free before bathing him, as bathing can tighten mats and make them more difficult or even impossible to brush out. If you do not brush your Poodle regularly, his coat will mat and the only way to remove the mats will be to shave him. When shaved, a matted Poodle coat will likely come off in one piece, similar to when sheep are shorn. Mats can be uncomfortable or even painful, especially in delicate areas such as the armpits and groin. In extreme cases, mats can become so tight that they restrict blood flow to the legs, ears, or tail. Luckily, mats are preventable with frequent and thorough brushing. Most experts recommend daily brushing, but some Poodles can be brushed three to four times per week with no problems. How often you brush your dog will depend on his individual coat, as well as his age, as puppies who are changing coats will need more frequent brushing.

When brushing your Poodle, it's best to use a combination of tools. Pin brushes and slicker brushes work well for large areas, but combs are useful for delicate areas as well as to check your work throughout the coat. Be sure to brush firmly enough that you are brushing more than just the surface of the coat, but not so firmly that you scratch your dog's skin with the brush. Poodles with longer coats can be "line brushed" which means that you part the coat into sections, or lines, as you brush, to make sure that every part of the dog is tangle-free. After brushing, you can use a metal comb to check that you've brushed the coat down to the skin. Metal combs are also useful for detangling and removing smaller mats. If you encounter mats that you can't remove with a comb, you may need to use a mat remover. Use caution, as mat removers use blades to cut out the mats and can cut your dog's skin if you aren't careful. If you have any doubts or questions about brushing your dog, ask your local groomer for a recommendation on tools and a demonstration on proper brushing techniques.

When bathing your Poodle, it's crucial that you make sure the dog is completely mat-free before shampooing. Shampooing, especially with warm water, can tighten mats and make them harder to remove. It's also important that you wash the dog down to the skin and rinse him thoroughly. Choose a shampoo that contains more natural ingredients. The fewer chemicals in the shampoo, the less likely your dog is to have a reaction. Shampoos without chemicals may produce less bubbles, so if your shampoo isn't as sudsy as you'd expect, don't worry, your dog is still getting clean.

No matter what type of shampoo you use, be careful when washing your dog's face. You want to keep the shampoo out of his ears, eyes, and nose. Once you've scrubbed your dog and are sure that you've reached the skin, it's time to rinse. Shampoo left in the coat can cause irritation and itching so it's important to rinse thoroughly. A good rule of thumb is when you think you've gotten all of the soap out, rinse one more time just to be sure.

Professional groomers use high-velocity dryers to dry the majority of the dogs they work with. With Poodles, this is an important step of the grooming process. Drying a curly coat with a high-velocity dryer or brushing the coat as it dries under a low-velocity dryer will help to straighten the coat. The result will be the fluffy, luxurious look you see in the show ring. Without a dryer, a Poodle's coat will dry in especially tight curls. If you do not use a dryer after bathing your Poodle, it's important to brush him thoroughly once his coat dries. Otherwise, his curls may develop mats, especially if he has a longer coat.

Photo Courtesy of
Lonnie Clay

Clipping

HELPFUL TIP
Brushing is Crucial

Unless you keep your Poodle in the shortest of kennel clips, you will need to brush it at least a few times a week. The longer you keep the hair on your Poodle, the more frequently you will need to brush it since the breed's curly fur becomes matted quite easily. Your Poodle will also need to be groomed every four to six weeks, which can be expensive, especially for larger dogs.

If you've never clipped a dog yourself before, it may be worthwhile to have a professional groom your dog for his first few haircuts. This will give you an idea of what your dog should look like after being clipped, but the groomer will also be able to get your dog used to the process. A nervous groomer and a nervous puppy are a recipe for disaster, so it's best to start on a dog who knows what to expect from the process. You may want to ask a professional groomer for advice on the best techniques to use on a Poodle. Your dog's breeder may also be able to give you advice on clipping your Poodle at home. Grooming is a skill that can take years to develop, so don't be disappointed if your first few haircuts don't look like a professional job.

Never use your clippers on a dirty coat. Even if your dog isn't covered in mud, the dust and dander in an unwashed coat can cause unnecessary wear and tear on your blades, reducing their life span. Clipper blades can last a long time if they are properly cared for, so be sure to take good care of them. As you clip your dog, check the blades every so often to see if they are getting hot. A hot blade can burn your Poodle's delicate skin. If your blade becomes hot quickly, you may be working with a dull or dirty blade, so it may be time to clean or sharpen your tools. Cleaning and oiling your blades after every use will also help them last longer.

When clipping your Poodle, use a gentle hand and light pressure. Too much pressure can force the dog's skin into the blades and you may cut him. This is especially important in delicate places such as the face and feet. Most groomers recommend clipping with the grain of the hair, rather than against it. For especially close clips on the face and feet, you may need to go against the grain, but for the dog's body and legs, going with the grain is best. As you clip, you may find that brushing the hair against the grain and going over it again with the clippers will result in a smoother, more even clip. Use extreme caution when clipping areas with thin skin such as the groin and ears. Never clip against the grain of the hair in these areas. The delicate skin is incredibly easy to cut if you aren't careful.

Different Hairstyles

The most well-known Poodle hairstyle is the continental clip. This is the extravagant style you see in the show ring. It's one of two acceptable styles for adult Poodles competing in conformation. The face, feet, hind end, legs, and tail are shaved closely, with the exception of poms on the ankles, hips, and end of the tail. The poms on the hips are often referred to as rosettes. The chest, neck, and head area of the dog are long and scissored into shape, rather than clipped. The hair on the dog's head, known as the topknot, is pulled into a ponytail.

The English Saddle Clip is the other style that is allowed in the show ring for adult Poodles. The front half of the dog is trimmed similarly to the continental clip. The tail and ankle poms are also the same, but there are additional poms on the dog's knees. Instead of the hip rosettes of the continental clip, this area is trimmed into a sort of short blanket shape.

For puppies under a year old, the only style accepted in the conformation ring is the puppy clip. This is also the most popular style for pet Poodles. With this style, the face, feet, and base of tail are shaved closely, much like with continental and English Saddle clips. The dog's body is trimmed to roughly the same length all over. The dog's topknot is long and rounded and the ears are left long but tidy.

The sporting clip is also a popular style for pet and sporting dogs. It's one of the more low-maintenance clips because the hair is kept shorter

than in the other styles. The face, feet, and base of the tail are clipped closely, and the dog's topknot is trimmed to an appropriate length. The rest of the body and legs are trimmed to the same length, usually less than an inch long. This clip is ideal for owners who don't want to spend hours brushing their dog each week. This clip is not allowed in the conformation ring, but is acceptable for Poodles competing in other sports.

Another popular and relatively low-maintenance style for pet Poodles is the lamb clip. As with other styles, the dog's face, feet, and base of the tail are clipped short. The dog's topknot is rounded and long enough to balance out the rest of the dog's body. The body is clipped closely and the legs are left longer so that they resemble sturdy columns. The difference in lengths is blended so that the coat appears smooth with no harsh lines.

With Poodles, there is no limit on the creativity you can express through your dog's haircut. Some owners choose to keep the ears closely clipped, while other prefer long ears. There are even different styles of moustaches that you can try out on your dog. Unless you are competing in conformation, you can clip your Poodle into any style that works for you. The texture of the Poodle's coat even allows it to develop cords, similar to breeds such as the Komondor and Puli, so if you are looking for a unique style you may want to try cording your dog's coat. Corded Poodles can also compete in conformation, as long as their cords adhere to the continental or English Saddle clips.

Photo Courtesy of Anita Wright

Trimming the Nails

There are two methods of trimming your Poodle's nails and which one you choose will be based on what works best for you and your dog. Traditional scissor-style nail clippers are the more popular method. Most groomers and veterinarians discourage owners from using guillotine-style nail clippers because they can crush and damage the nail. Nail clippers are easy to use and come in different sizes for different-size dogs. The downside to nail clippers is that you can inadvertently cut the nail's blood supply, or quick, rather easily if you aren't careful. The other method of nail trimming is to use a nail grinder. Nail grinders are a small electric tool that grinds your dog's nails down just a layer at a time. This can make it easier to keep an eye on the nail's quick to make sure you don't go too short. Grinders also make it possible to round off the dog's nails, reducing the chances of you or your furniture getting scratched. The downside is that the grinder's spinning head can easily grab hold of a Poodle's long hair, so care must be taken to keep the hair out of the way. Some dogs are uncomfortable with the noise and feel of the grinder and some don't like the pressure on their nails from the clippers, so you may want to try both methods to see which one your dog prefers.

Before you trim your Poodle's nails, take a look to see if you can locate the quick inside the nail. If your dog has dark or black nails, you may not be able to see it. If you can see the quick, take note of how far down the nail it extends and try not to cut this far into the nail when you trim it. You'll also want to make sure that your Poodle is adequately restrained before you start, especially if this is a new experience for him. A wiggly Poodle is difficult to trim and can hurt himself or you. An elevated surface may also make things easier for you, especially with Toy and Miniature Poodles. A grooming table with an arm and lead is ideal. Regardless of the method used, when you take your dog's paw, brush back any hair that could get caught or make it difficult to see. With your grinder or clipper, take just a small layer off the nail at a time, rather than one big cut. As you trim, you may begin to see a dark circle developing in the center of the nail. When you see this dark circle, stop trimming. This is the end of the quick and if you cut any further, you will find blood. If your dog is new to nail trimming and has stood patiently for you, praise and reward him. You want to make this a positive experience so he'll behave again in the future.

Your Poodle's nails will need to be trimmed regularly, but the exact time frame will differ depending on how fast his nails grow and where you walk him. Dogs who are walked on pavement will often grind their nails down enough that they don't need trimmed that often. Dogs who exercise

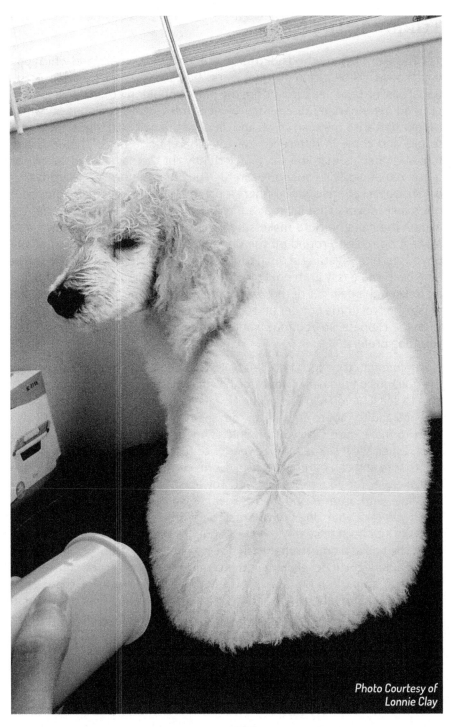

Photo Courtesy of Lonnie Clay

on soft surfaces such as sand or grass may need more frequent nail trims. Some owners choose to trim their dogs every week or two, while other do it monthly. It's up to you how often you trim your dog's nails, but keep in mind that long nails can have an impact on the dog's ability to walk comfortably, so be sure to keep them at an appropriate length. If you are struggling to trim your dog's nails yourself, you may want to take him to your vet or groomer for regular trims or ask them for advice. Nail trims are typically quite inexpensive, so many owners just opt to have someone else do it for them.

Brushing their Teeth

As with your own teeth, the only real way to make a difference is to brush them daily. Daily brushing will help prevent the buildup of plaque and tartar and increase the length of time between professional dental cleanings. Excess tartar can cause painful inflammation in your dog's gums and release harmful bacteria into his bloodstream. He can develop painful abscesses, leading to tooth loss and systemic infections. However, periodontal disease is easily preventable with regular at-home dental care. With practice, the process of brushing your dog's teeth will only take a few minutes and can easily fit into the busiest of daily routines.

You will find a variety of toothbrushes and toothpastes at your local pet store or favorite online retailer. Toothbrushes come in a range of sizes and shapes to suit every type of dog. Most doggy toothpastes are flavored to encourage them to tolerate and even enjoy the process. Try out a few different types to see what works best for you and your dog. You may prefer silicone toothbrushes that slip over your finger, or you may want one that's shaped more like your own toothbrush. Your dog may not enjoy getting his teeth brushed at first, but with consistency and positive reinforcement, he will learn to stand or sit patiently while you work.

Even if you brush your dog's teeth daily, he will still need to see his veterinarian for professional dental cleanings. Most vets recommend cleanings every six to 12 months. Small dogs have a tendency to build up tartar more quickly than larger dogs, so Toy and Miniature Poodles may need more frequent cleanings than Standard Poodles. Your dog's diet and whether he chews on toys or treats will also affect how often he needs his teeth cleaned. It's best to ask your veterinarian for specific advice on your dog's dental care schedule.

Cleaning Ears and Eyes

Poodles can be prone to ear infections because of their long, hanging ears and the hair that often grows in the ear canal. Moisture can have a huge impact on your dog's ears so be sure to clean his ears after every bath or swim. Some groomers and vets also recommend plucking the hair from the ear canal to aid in the circulation of air in the ear. If you notice your dog scratching at his ears, or his ears appear to be red or swollen, it may be time to visit your veterinarian. A simple ear swab will tell your vet whether the infection is due to yeast or bacteria. Treatment usually consists of an ear wash, medication, and possibly antibiotics.

When choosing an ear cleaner, avoid cleaners that include alcohol. Alcohol can cause a burning sensation, especially on inflamed, irritated ears. Soak a cotton ball in your chosen ear cleaner and squeeze out the excess. Use the wet cotton ball to wipe around your dog's ear canal. Use your finger to wipe the cotton ball as far down your dog's ear canal as you can without hurting him. Your finger is too large to do any damage, so as long as you are gentle, you shouldn't hurt your dog. If his ear is infected, he may be more sensitive, so you may need to be extra gentle. Do not use cotton swabs as they are small enough to reach deep into ear and you may seriously injure your dog's ears. Be sure to wipe up any excess cleaner with a dry cotton ball when you are done.

Some Poodles, especially Toys, are prone to tearstains under the eyes. Larger Poodles can also develop tearstains, but they are more common in small dogs. Tearstains are caused by an overgrowth of yeast and you may notice reddish-brown discoloration and an unpleasant smell. Although there's no way to completely prevent tearstains, they are easy to manage. Clipping your Poodle's face short can help, but so can regular cleaning. Shampooing this close to your dog's eyes is not a good idea, but there are plenty of safe products to use in this area. As with ear cleaning, wet a cotton ball in your chosen eye cleaner and simply wipe away the moisture below your dog's eyes. Frequent cleaning will prevent yeast buildup and reduce the staining and odor.

When Professional Help is Necessary

Professional help is available whenever you want it. If you don't want to do any of your dog's grooming and your budget allows, you can have a professional groomer bathe, brush, and clip your dog. If you'd rather do everything yourself, you can also ask a professional for guidance on the proper products and techniques. You may find that you don't mind brushing your dog at home, but the thought of clipping him makes you uncomfortable. Plenty of Poodle owners would rather have someone else do the dirty work of caring for their dog's coats, so don't be afraid to give your local groomer a call.

Groomers are also experienced with difficult dogs. They know how to calm an anxious dog and get the job done with a gentle touch. Many groomers welcome difficult dogs because they know that they can gain the dog's trust, and after a few grooms they become much easier to handle. It can be helpful to take your dog to the same groomer every time, so they can develop a relationship. Your dog may be a bit nervous the first couple time he visits the groomer, but soon he'll be excited to see his new friend and be pampered.

CHAPTER 16
Basic Health Care

Visiting the Vet

Routine veterinary care is essential to your Poodle's overall health and well-being. Most veterinarians recommend a physical exam every six to 12 months. Young puppies and senior dogs may need to be seen more frequently than healthy adult dogs. It may seem unnecessary to pay for such frequent vet visits, but it's important to catch any health concerns in the early stages before they become serious or life-threatening. Your dog will also need to see the vet regularly for vaccinations and deworming. For many owners, the only time their dog gets weighed is at the vet, so this is also an opportunity to discuss your dog's weight and diet with your veterinarian. If you have any questions about your dog's health or behavior, regular vet visits give you the opportunity to seek professional advice when you need it.

Fleas and Ticks

Fleas and ticks are a common source of disease for both dogs and humans. They are especially dangerous because they can wreak havoc on the health of your pets and your human family members. Fleas often carry tapeworms and Bartonellosis and are a common cause of anemia. Flea dermatitis, which is a result of your dog's immune system reacting to the fleas' saliva, can also cause severe itching, skin inflammation, and hair loss. In addition to Lyme disease, ticks can carry Rocky Mountain spotted fever, ehrlichiosis, and babesiosis, all of which can be transmitted to humans. Regular flea and tick prevention is crucial in maintaining the health of your Poodle and your family.

Depending on the area in which you live, flea and tick prevention may or may not be recommended year-round. Climates with especially cold winter may not require treatment during the colder months, but more mild climates may require you to treat your dog all year long. Talk to your veterinarian about how often you should be treating your dog for fleas and ticks. Some boarding facilities require dogs to receive treatment before they are allowed to stay, so if you board your dog frequently, talk to the staff to see what their specific requirements are. They may be on the same page as your veterinarian, or they may require year-round treatment no matter what.

One of the most popular methods of flea and tick prevention is the application of topical drops. This type of treatment is packaged in a plastic vial, which will break on one end, allowing the product to be released. Simply part the hair on the back of the dog's neck and squirt the vial directly on to the skin. Be sure to apply the product to the skin, not the hair. It's typically applied to the back of the neck to prevent the dog from licking it off. Topical flea and tick prevention is usually applied once a month and your veterinarian will be able to recommend which brand will work best for your dog. Like most medications, topical flea and tick prevention can have side effects, so if you have any concerns about your Poodle, talk to your veterinarian before applying any product. Side effects can include tremors, seizures, vomiting, lethargy, and skin irritation.

Flea and tick collars are another option, but you must use caution, especially if you are a multi-pet household. Some flea collars contain harsh chemicals, such as tetrachlorvinphos, which can cause serious and even fatal reactions in cats. Some dogs also experience skin irritation, vomiting, and even seizures. The Environmental Protection Agency considers tetrachlorvinphos to be carcinogenic, so you may want to avoid it entirely for the sake of yourself and your human family members.

Worms and Parasites

Unfortunately, external parasites are not the only creatures that can impact your Poodle's health. Intestinal worms and other parasites can cause serious illness if they aren't treated as soon as possible. The specific parasites that your dog is at risk of ingesting will vary according to your location, but if you suspect your dog may be infected, take him to your veterinarian as soon as possible. Many intestinal parasites can be passed on to humans, so the sooner your dog can be treated, the better.

Intestinal worms are common in dogs of all breeds and sizes. Puppies are especially prone to ingesting worms because they often explore the world with their mouths. Worms are usually passed on from one animal to another through the ingestion of contaminated food, water, soil, and feces. If a mother dog is infected, she can also pass worms on to her puppies before they are born or through her milk. Roundworms, whipworms, tapeworms, and hookworms are the most common intestinal parasites in dogs. Protozoa such as giardia and coccidia are also common and can pass from one dog to another quite easily. In warm climates, heartworm is also a concern. Heartworm is carried by mosquitoes and is passed from one host to the next through a mosquito's bites. Heartworms live in the dog's heart and serious infections can clog a dog's arteries, leading to death. Heartworm is a more difficult infection to treat since care must be taken to kill the worms slowly to prevent dead worms from blocking the flow of blood through the dog's body. Luckily, internal parasite infections are easy to treat and can even be prevented with regular deworming.

HELPFUL TIP
Don't Forget the Teeth

Did you know that improper dental hygiene can lead to heart disease in your Poodle? Without regular toothbrushing, bacteria can grow under your dog's gumline until it eventually reaches your dog's bloodstream, where it can reach the organs, including the heart. Brushing your dog's teeth should become a part of your daily routine, as should regular cleanings under sedation from your veterinarian.

Your Poodle may be infected by an internal parasite if you notice any significant changes in his weight, vomiting, diarrhea, or lethargy. Dogs with heavy parasitic loads may also be severely anemic. Some dogs, especially puppies, may appear to have a distended abdomen with an otherwise thin or malnourished-looking body. Some dogs, especially those in the early stages of infection, may show no symptoms at all. If you pay close attention to your dog's bathroom habits, you may notice evidence of intestinal worms in his feces.

Photo Courtesy of
Nick and Krysta Ventriglio

If you suspect your Poodle may have an internal parasite problem, take him to your vet as soon as possible. Your vet will be able to take a fecal sample to examine under a microscope to determine which type of worm your dog is carrying. The eggs and larvae of worms are easily detectable under a high-powered microscope. Heartworm is detectable through a simple blood test. After your veterinarian determines what type of parasite is affecting your dog, a treatment can be prescribed. Most parasites can be killed with either an oral medication or an injection. Particularly heavy parasite loads may take several weeks to cure, while heartworm can take several months. With regular testing and deworming, serious infections can be prevented.

Holistic Alternatives and Supplements

Photo Courtesy of Jessica Minnen

If you are the type of person who prefers more natural methods of healing, consider searching for a holistic veterinarian in your area. Holistic veterinary medicine allows practitioners to combine modern conventional medicine with alternative therapies. Holistic veterinarians are as qualified as any other type of vet to perform conventional surgeries and treatments, but they may supplement these therapies with acupuncture, chiropractic adjustments, or herbal or nutritional therapy. If your Poodle suffers from a chronic condition, such as arthritis or heart disease, he may be a great candidate for some type of alternative therapy. If your dog has an accident and needs emergency surgery, obviously conventional medicine is the way to go, but for chronic conditions, it's often not a bad idea to search for different types of treatment.

Holistic medicine treats your pet's body as a whole, rather than individual parts or systems. For example, if your Poodle suffers from arthritis, a holistic veterinarian may choose a combination of nutritional supplements, chiropractic adjustments, or acupuncture. The problem may be specific to certain joints, but the vet will address the dog's overall health and well-being in an effort to improve a specific condition.

The American Holistic Veterinary Medical Association has a searchable list on their website of all certified holistic veterinarians in the United States and Canada. You can search by the specialty of the vet or the types of treatment offered. Many vets specialize in certain types of animals or therapies and the website allows you to narrow your search and find the perfect holistic veterinarian for your Poodle.

Vaccinations

Your Poodle, like any other dog, will require a certain number of vaccinations throughout his life. Most dogs start with a series of vaccinations as puppies, then receive regular boosters throughout their adulthood. Vaccines for the most common diseases, such as rabies and parvovirus, are considered core vaccines because they offer the broadest protection for the majority of dogs. Non-core vaccines protect dogs from less common diseases, such as leptospirosis or kennel cough, and are generally recommended on an as-needed basis. Some diseases are more prevalent in certain areas, so your veterinarian will be able to recommend which vaccines your Poodle should have and how often.

Core vaccines are usually combined into one shot to reduce the stress on your dog and eliminate the need for an excessive number of injections. Instead of multiple injections, the antibodies for several different diseases are combined in a single syringe. The most common vaccine, often referred to as a five-way, or DHPP, protects dogs against parvovirus, distemper, adenovirus cough, parainfluenza, and hepatitis. Seven-way vaccines are also available which protect against the previously mentioned diseases as well as leptospirosis and coronavirus. As puppies, dogs receive a series of three vaccines, usually at six, 12, and 16 weeks of age. Thereafter, dogs will be vaccinated once a year or once every three years, depending on the recommendation of your vet.

The rabies vaccine is the only core vaccine that is required by law. Your Poodle should receive his first rabies vaccine at around 16 weeks of age. The next rabies shot is given one year after the first. If the dog is kept current on his rabies vaccination, he may receive additional vaccinations once per year or once every three years. The frequency will depend on your veterinarian's recommendation and the area you live in.

Common non-core vaccines protect dogs against leptospirosis, Lyme disease, kennel cough, and rattlesnake venom. Your vet may or may not recommend non-core vaccines, and it may vary by location. Non-core vaccines do not offer long-term protection like core vaccines do. Additionally, they may not be as effective, especially against various strains of the diseases. Many boarding facilities, vet clinics, and doggy day cares require dogs to be vaccinated against kennel cough, also known as Bordetella, so if you frequently board your dog, he may need to be vaccinated prior to dropping him off. Some vets recommend against non-core vaccines, simply because their efficacy hasn't been proven, but some vets will recommend vaccinating against anything and everything. It's important to discuss your

Poodle's specific needs with your veterinarian to determine which vaccines are best for him.

It's not uncommon for Poodles to experience allergic reactions to vaccines. Smaller dogs, such as Toy Poodles, are especially prone to reactions. Unfortunately, vaccines only come in one size, so a tiny Toy Poodle puppy is going to receive the same amount of antibodies as an adult Great Dane. Many Poodle owners only give their dogs one vaccine at a time to limit the possibility of an allergic reaction. For instance, if your Poodle is due for DHPP and rabies, you may want to give him one vaccine this visit and come back a week or two later for the second vaccine. Symptoms of an allergic reaction include swelling of the face or paws, hives, lethargy, vomiting, and pain or swelling at the injection site. If your dog experiences difficulty breathing or seizures, he needs to see a vet immediately. If your dog shows any reaction after vaccinations, take him back to the vet as soon as possible. Even if the reaction isn't life-threatening, your vet still needs to know about the severity of your dog's reaction. It can be helpful to wait at the vet clinic for 15-20 minutes after vaccinations to make sure your dog doesn't react, so if your Poodle is particularly sensitive and you have the time, it will save you from having to drive back to the clinic.

Adult dogs who have already received their puppyhood vaccines may undergo titer testing. Most vets offer titer testing, even if they don't advertise it, so if this is something you're interested in, talk to your veterinarian.

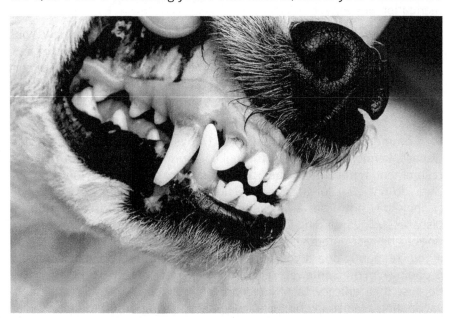

Titer testing measures the antibodies in your dog's blood to see if they are at a high enough level to protect the dog against disease. If the levels are sufficient, the dog doesn't need to be vaccinated. If the levels are too low, the dog will need to receive another vaccine. Titer testing can only be done for core vaccines, as non-core vaccines do not last long enough to protect for a significant period of time. Titer testing is a relatively simple procedure. Your vet will draw a sample of your dog's blood and if they do not have the equipment in their clinic, they will ship the sample to an outside laboratory for testing. Although titer testing can be more expensive than regular vaccines, if you have a sensitive Poodle or simply do not want to over-vaccinate your dog, it may be a good alternative to yearly vaccinations.

Pet Insurance

Veterinary health care is usually not quite as expensive as human health care, but in an emergency, the cost for your Poodle's care can skyrocket. Pet insurance is a popular choice for owners on a budget who want to be prepared in case of emergencies. Like human health insurance, different companies offer different levels of coverage at different rates. You can choose your dog's plan according your preferred monthly premium or level of coverage. If your dog has any preexisting conditions, coverage may be denied, or premiums may be quite high.

Most pet insurance policies do not cover routine care. Yearly health exams, vaccinations, and dental cleanings will likely be paid for out-of-pocket. There are companies that offer coverage for these services, but premiums may be quite expensive. Some veterinary clinics also offer plans that cover all routine care, with a monthly fee, of course, so you can always supplement your dog's insurance plan if necessary. If your Poodle is seriously injured in an accident or is diagnosed with a chronic condition, pet insurance can help cover the cost of treatment.

Many dog owners will gladly pay a monthly premium to know that their dog is covered in case of an accident, but many others don't think it's worth the money. For a healthy Poodle who remains accident-free for the majority of his life, it may just be a waste of money. Instead of spending the money on an insurance plan, many owners choose to put a small amount of money away each month in order to save up for any emergency treatments. If you're curious about pet insurance, it's important for you to do your research to determine if it's a good choice for your individual situation.

CHAPTER 17
Advanced Poodle Health and Aging Dog Care

Common Diseases and Conditions in Poodles

Periodontal disease is a common affliction for Toy and Miniature Poodles. Smaller dogs are simply more prone to dental problems than larger dogs. Smaller Poodles may need more frequent dental cleanings than Standard Poodles. Without proper care, periodontal disease can lead to tooth loss and potentially life-threatening systemic infections. Regular visits with your veterinarian and a properly balanced diet can make a tremendous difference in your dog's dental health.

Photo Courtesy of Juan Barrionuevo

Bloat is a common condition affecting deep-chested breeds such as Standard Poodles. Sometimes referred to as gastric dilation volvulus or gastric torsion, bloat can be fatal if not treated immediately. In some cases, the stomach swells with gas but does not twist, but if torsion does occur, it cuts off necessary blood supply to the organs and other tissues. Dogs who gulp their food down, eat large meals, or exercise immediately after eating may be more prone to bloat. Symptoms may include abdominal swelling, dry heaving, drooling, restlessness, and rapid breathing and heart rate. If you notice any of these symptoms, take your dog to the vet immediately. Although not completely preventable, you can take steps to reduce the chances of bloat. Feeding your dog smaller meals throughout the day and limiting exercise for at least an hour after eating can help reduce the likelihood of bloat. If your dog gulps his food, try a specially designed bowl to help slow him down. Some diets are also linked to higher rates of bloat, so talk to your veterinarian about the steps you can take to prevent gastric torsion.

Genetic Traits Found in Poodles

Progressive retinal atrophy, or PRA, is a common genetic condition found in Toy and Miniature Poodles. Although PRA is not painful, it can cause a dog to completely lose all sight. Often, the first signs of PRA are night blindness and dilated pupils. Eventually, the dog's sight will deteriorate to the point of total blindness. Although the disease is not curable, there are treatments that can slow the degeneration of the structures of the eye. Unfortunately, the disease progresses quickly, and many dogs can become completely blind within a year of the first symptoms.

Patellar luxation is often found in Toy and Miniature Poodles. This condition affects the stifle, or knee joints, of the back legs. In a normal dog, the patella, or kneecap, sits in a groove in the femur, or thigh bone. In dogs with patellar luxation, the kneecap will slip out of place, sliding to the side of the groove. There are varying levels of severity, but in the more serious cases the kneecap will stay to the side of the groove at all times. If your dog has luxating patellas, you may notice him "skipping." This action often adjusts the kneecap back into place, so dogs quickly learn to adjust their gait accordingly. It can be a painful condition if not treated, and the only treatment is surgery.

Hip dysplasia is another common ailment in Miniature and Standard Poodles. In normal dogs, the hip joint is a ball and socket that slides smoothly during movement. In dogs with hip dysplasia, the ball and socket do not fit together neatly and may grind or rub, rather than the smooth sliding action of a healthy joint. Over time, this grinding can lead to deterioration of

Photo Courtesy of Tony Austin

the joint and eventual loss of mobility. Some dogs develop a sort of "bunny hop" to their gait to ease their pain. Other symptoms include decreased activity or range of motion, loss of thigh muscle mass, or stiffness in the rear end. Milder cases can be treated with nutritional supplements and lifestyle modifications, but more serious cases may require surgery.

Sebaceous adenitis is a common condition affecting Standard Poodles, but it can be found in smaller Poodles as well. Also known as SA, the disease affects the sebaceous glands of the skin, which become inflamed. This inflammation can eventually lead to a progressive loss of hair. The initial symptoms can include excessive dandruff, hair loss, lesions, and a bad odor. Some dogs, however, show no symptoms at all. Although it is typically inherited from parent dogs, there is no DNA test available to test for SA. Diagnosis depends on skin biopsies and testing. The disease is not curable, but any secondary skin infections can be treated and certain grooming products can also help with skin condition.

For most genetic conditions, prevention is only possible through consistent health testing by breeders. Terri L. Creech of Bear Cove Standard Poodles says, "Health testing is critical for producing healthy dogs. It's no guarantee that something will not affect the puppy later in life, but the health testing reduces the risk." Reputable breeders are passionate about the breed and work continuously to improve the health and quality of life of their dogs. By testing each and every dog before it's bred, they can help reduce the chances of the puppies inheriting these common conditions.

Illness and Injury Prevention

It's impossible to completely prevent your Poodle from falling ill or getting injured, but there are a few things that can be done to reduce the likelihood of a tragedy. Properly managing your dog's daily routine and scheduling regular veterinary examinations can make a huge difference in your dog's overall health and well-being. Poodles are smart, athletic dogs and they can easily find their way into a bad situation, so you must be cautious about your dog's surroundings. Smaller Poodles can easily be injured by larger playmates, Standard Poodles can be injured chasing after rabbits, and all Poodles can be hurt if they are allowed to run free in inappropriate places. This does not mean you need to keep your dog at home, away from the world, but you should use common sense when entering into new situations. Regular veterinary care will also help prevent any serious health problems. The sooner your vet can detect a problem, the sooner treatment can be prescribed. It's your responsibility as a pet owner to manage your dog to prevent serious injury.

Basics of Senior Dog Care

Most experts suggest that dogs are typically considered to be senior at around eight years of age. This doesn't mean that your dog suddenly becomes geriatric on his eighth birthday. Smaller dogs, such as Toy and Miniature Poodles, usually have a longer life span, so they may begin to exhibit the signs of old age later in life than a Standard Poodle would. If your Poodle suffers from certain health conditions, he may begin to slow down much earlier than the age of eight. Likewise, if he's healthy and reasonably fit, he may not begin to exhibit signs of aging until later in life. Age will affect each dog differently, but it's important to keep an eye out and adjust your dog's lifestyle accordingly.

Your Poodle's body and behavior may change as he ages. These changes can be quite slow, or they may seem to happen rather rapidly. You might notice that your Poodle spends more time sleeping and less time chasing squirrels in the backyard. He may seem stiff getting up after a nap or he may tire more quickly during his daily walks. Some dogs may experience a deterioration of their sight or hearing. You may notice your Poodle bumping into things or responding less to your verbal commands. If your Poodle seems to be losing his sight or hearing, it's crucial that you use a little more

Photo Courtesy of Matthew Fisher

caution, especially when approaching your dog from behind or when he's sleeping. A startled dog may snap, even if he has never been an aggressive dog in the past. Many older dogs gain weight, but there are some that have trouble keeping weight on. Older dogs also have less control over their bladders, so they may need to go out more frequently or they may have accidents in the house. It's also possible for older dogs to develop symptoms of cognitive disfunction, or dementia, so you may notice your senior Poodle acting confused from time to time. Each dog experiences aging differently, but it's up to you to notice the signs and adjust his care accordingly.

Grooming

HELPFUL TIP

Grooming Needs May Change

One thing many people don't consider as their Poodle ages is that grooming needs may change. If your Poodle develops arthritis, for example, is it really fair to force your pet to stand while the groomer shaves its feet, which can take anywhere from 10-30 minutes for all four feet? Haircuts may need to change and simplify as your dog ages to keep it comfortable during and after the grooming process. Ask your regular groomer if they would change anything about your senior Poodle's haircut for the comfort of your aging dog.

As your Poodle ages, you may need to make adjustments to his grooming needs. Whether they're done by you or a professional, regular grooming sessions are a great way to check your dog's skin and coat. Older dogs often develop lumps, bumps, and hair thinning or loss as they age, and each grooming session is an opportunity to track the changes in the overall health of your dog's skin and coat.

Older Poodles often require more patience and different handling techniques. Many older dogs have difficulty standing for an entire grooming session, so their groomer may need to give them breaks as they become tired. Dogs who are showing signs of dementia may become frightened or try to bite, even if they have always been well-behaved in the past. Senior Poodles may have painful joints that need to be handled more cautiously than before. It's also common for older Poodles to have thinner, more delicate skin, so more caution may be needed when brushing and clipping certain areas.

Many Poodle owners choose to groom their senior dogs in less extravagant hairstyles as they age. Since older dogs typically can't tolerate long grooming sessions anymore, it may be necessary to change their hairstyle to a more functional cut. Longer hairstyles are also more prone to matting if they aren't taken care of properly. Older Poodles may have more delicate skin, or simply not enough patience to tolerate long de-matting or brushing sessions. Some Poodles may also require different types of shampoo or conditioner as they age, to accommodate more sensitive or dry skin. With each grooming, take a close look at your Poodle's skin and coat and make the necessary adjustments to keep him looking and feeling his best.

Nutrition

Many older Poodles need to have their diets changed slightly as they go through the aging process. As their metabolism slows down, their caloric intake will need to be adjusted accordingly to prevent excess weight gain. Excess weight can be especially hard on arthritic joints, so it's essential that you keep your senior Poodle at a healthy weight. Most senior dog foods contain less calories per cup than those formulated for puppies and adults. Not all senior dogs will gain weight as they age. There are many senior dogs who struggle to keep weight on. They may appear rather thin and frail, but they might be perfectly healthy. If you notice any sudden changes in your dog's weight or appetite, it's important that you seek advice from your veterinarian as soon as possible. Changes in weight or appetite may just be signs of aging, but they could also be signs of serious health conditions.

If your Poodle has developed various health conditions as he's gotten older, you may need to make changes to diet according to his specific condition. Dogs who suffer from diabetes, or heart or kidney disease may need a certain type of food to treat their ailment. Many foods that are used to treat chronic conditions are only available from a veterinarian. Prescription dog food can be expensive, but it can also make a big difference in the overall health of your pet.

As your Poodle ages, you may also want to consider adding certain nutritional supplements to his diet. It's common for older dogs to take a daily dose of glucosamine and chondroitin sulfate to help ease their joint pain. Some older dogs may also need additional fiber or probiotics added to their diet to help with age-related digestive issues. Senior dogs who have lost their appetite may also need something added to their food to entice them to eat. Bone broth, warm water, or canned food are excellent choices. Before you add any supplements to your Poodle's diet, you need to discuss it with your vet to make sure you are making the right choices.

Exercise

As your Poodle ages, his slowing metabolism and arthritic joints may cause him to slow down. Even the most rambunctious Poodle will slow down as he gets older. However, regular exercise should still be an important part of your dog's daily routine. Not only is it essential to your dog's physical and mental health, but it's an important part of proper weight management as well. Obesity can put excess strain on your dog's joints, discouraging him from exercising. This lack of exercise can lead to further weight gain, which can eventually have a huge impact on your dog's quality of life during his senior years.

Although you should never eliminate exercise from your senior dog's daily routine, you may need to make some adjustments. Slick surfaces or steep stairs and inclines can be difficult to manage for many older dogs. Rather than a high-energy game of fetch, your dog might now prefer a leisurely stroll through the neighborhood. As your dog's mobility becomes affected by the symptoms of old age, you may want to offer more opportunities for mental stimulation rather than physical. Puzzle toys or scent work are great ways to keep your dog's mind exercised without putting too much strain on his aging body.

Common Old-age Ailments

Arthritis is one of the most common ailments affecting Poodles of all sizes. You may notice your dog having difficulty getting up after naps or becoming stiff after his daily walks. Many older dogs may also begin to lose their sight or hearing. As with humans, older dogs may also exhibit signs of memory loss or confusion and they may startle more easily. Instead of the long, strenuous exercise sessions of their youth, many older Poodles prefer to sleep most of the day and take only short walks. Incontinence is another common problem in older dogs. No matter what signs of aging your dog is exhibiting, it's your responsibility as his caretaker to make the necessary changes to his surroundings and his lifestyle to make him comfortable during your final years together.

When It's Time to Say Goodbye

One of the most difficult times in any Poodle owner's life is saying goodbye to their best friend. As you mourn the loss of your beloved companion, it's important to remember the joyful moments you have shared together. Reflect on your time together and be thankful that you had the opportunity to have your life touched by such a wonderful being.

As the end nears, it may be difficult to make the choice to say goodbye. In your grief, you may have difficulty making the necessary arrangements, but veterinary professionals will be there to help you every step of the way. Many veterinary clinics offer both in-office and at-home euthanasia services. Some dog owners would prefer not to have the memory of losing their beloved friend in their own home, while others would prefer that they say goodbye to their pet in familiar surroundings. Whatever you prefer, you should be able to find a supportive veterinary team to meet your needs. No matter where you choose to say goodbye, the most important thing is that he spends his final moments surrounded by people who love him.

Most veterinary clinics offer several different options for your dog's remains. If you would prefer not to deal with your Poodle's remains yourself, the veterinary team will be happy to take care of the disposal. They are experts in treating pets with respect and dignity, even after they have passed. Many clinics also offer cremation services, which gives you the opportunity to have the ashes returned to you if you wish. You may also have the choice of a variety of urns or a simple cardboard box. If you would prefer to discuss these details before the time comes, your veterinarian may be able to have everything planned out ahead of time.

Keeping your beloved Poodle's memory alive is often an important part of the grieving process. Many owners choose to create a memorial to help them treasure their fond memories. Personalized stones, tiles, or decorations are common choices. You can even have jewelry made from your dog's nose or paw prints. No matter how you choose to honor your Poodle's memory, remember the good times you had together and the unconditional love you gave and received.

Made in the USA
Monee, IL
05 June 2021